THE LAST ELIZABETHAN

BY CONSTANCE FECHER

Venture for a Crown

Heir to Pendarrow

Bright Star:
  A Portrait of Ellen Terry

The Link Boys

The Last Elizabethan:
  A Portrait of Sir Walter Ralegh

National Portrait Gallery

CONSTANCE FECHER

The Last Elizabethan

A PORTRAIT OF

Sir Walter Ralegh

FARRAR, STRAUS & GIROUX
NEW YORK

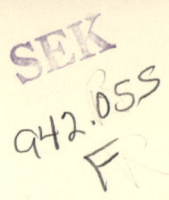

Copyright © 1972 by Constance Fecher
All rights reserved
Library of Congress catalog card number: 74-178882
ISBN 0-374-34361-6
First printing, 1972
Printed in the United States of America
Designed by Betty Crumley
Published simultaneously in Canada by Doubleday Canada Ltd., Toronto

For Michael and Angela

CONTENTS

    Preface xi
1 : *The Dawn and Rising Sun of Youth* 3
2 : *Fortune, my Foe* 15
3 : *I live to serve* 30
4 : *Dear Empress of my Heart* 40
5 : *To seek new worlds for gold, for praise, for glory* 49
6 : *That Morris Dance upon the Waters* 67
7 : *The Summer's Nightingale* 79
8 : *True Love is a durable Fire* 91
9 : *The great rich and beautiful empire of Guiana* 100
10 : *Now all the youth of England are on fire* 111
11 : *Sweet England's Pride Is Gone* 128
12 : *Leave Every Man Free* 136
13 : *My Death was Determined* 150
14 : *Despair bolts up my doors* 169
15 : *That Glorious Prince* 178
16 : *His Last Dream* 193
17 : *My Name hath lived among them* 203
18 : *A Star at which the World hath gazed* 217
    Bibliography 233
    Index 237

PREFACE

There is something legendary about Sir Walter Ralegh. You do not quite believe in him. He was courtier, soldier, seaman, poet, colonizer, scientist, historian, medicine man—it is too much. Even his contemporaries were puzzled by him. He was too clever, his ideas were too different from theirs, too far in advance of his time. They did not understand him, so they distrusted him, envied him, hated him.

Everyone has heard how as a young man he spent his last penny on a magnificent cloak and threw it in the mud before his queen's feet when she stepped off her barge at Greenwich.

Everyone has heard how he used the diamond in the hilt of his dagger to write on a windowpane: "Fain would I rise, yet fear to fall"; and Queen Elizabeth, reading it, wrote underneath: "If thy heart fail thee, rise not at all."

These are the tales, and though contemporary evidence does not support them, they could be true. The gesture of the cloak is typical of him. There was even a rumor that the pearls on it were so loosely sewn that they scattered as he walked and the people scrambled after them in the streets. Everything he did was touched with a splendid extravagance.

But how fascinating it is to look for the man behind the legends: the boy who set out from a humble home to gain high favor under a queen, only to lose it all under a king who hated him; the prisoner in the Tower who even in old age still pursued his dream, risking all he had in an impossible venture, and who died on the scaffold only to win imperishable glory.

The Elizabethans did not give much of themselves away. They did not keep diaries or write autobiographies or reveal their inner feelings. Their portraits show them, magnificently dressed against splendid backgrounds, with masklike faces that tell us little. One has to dig and probe to discover what they really felt. In some ways Ralegh revealed more of himself than did most of his contemporaries. All his life he was inclined to speak first and think afterward. His poetry, unlike most other Elizabethan verse, is intensely personal, written under the stress of deep and sincere feeling. Like all of us, he had faults. He was proud, quick-tempered, ambitious, and impatient of those less brilliant than he. Yet there is no record of him treating unjustly those who served him, and where he governed, he was admired and loved. Many of his letters and even his great *History of the World* have individual touches that reveal the man. From these I have tried to construct a portrait of a living person in place of a name in a history book.

Everything he put his hand to had sparkle and brilliance, and yet none of his ventures succeeded. He has been called a man of failure, and yet it is men such as he, far in advance of their time, who blaze a trail for others to follow. "I shall live to see Virginia an Empire yet," he said when he was imprisoned in the Tower, and so he did. Jamestown was not founded until 1612, but it was his pioneer voyages more than twenty years before that had made it possible.

In modern Venezuela, the Guiana of his time, they are today finding a great store of mineral wealth in the very place (where the river Orinoco meets the falls of the Caroni) where he and his men dug the stones out of the earth with their daggers. After nearly four hundred years the account he wrote of the riches of Guiana, which his fellow countrymen scoffed at, is being proved true.

I have not invented anything. Dialogue where it occurs is authentic or from reported speech in Elizabethan documents or extracted from letters and reports that reveal the writer's thoughts. The speeches at his trial are all to be found in the original record. His early life up to the campaign in Ireland is obscure and not well documented, but within the known facts, from what he himself wrote in later life, and from a knowledge of his times, it is possible to create a picture of a young man struggling against poverty with little to help him except his own genius.

A word about the spelling of his name: from 1581 he always signed himself *Ralegh*, as did his son and grandson until the end of the seventeenth century. The modern version—*Raleigh*—is the only one that neither he nor his family are ever known to have employed, and for this reason I have chosen to keep the form that he himself must have preferred.

THE LAST ELIZABETHAN

1 : "The Dawn and Rising Sun of Youth"

—Walter Ralegh

"Ye see that bit of black rock," said the seaman with the bushy brown beard, his red woolen cap pulled down over his head and silver rings glinting in his ears. "That's got gold in it, that has. You keep it in your pocket, Master Wat. It'll bring ye luck in those foreign parts where you're goin'."

The sailor called back a cheery farewell as he waded through the surf, climbed into the boat, and was rowed swiftly across the water to the waiting ship.

Walter Ralegh looked down at the black lump in his hand and wondered if it could be true. Then he climbed the rising crest of shingle and watched the fishing fleet move out on the evening tide. The sails were being run up. They billowed out in the breeze and the ships glided over the water to start their long voyage to Newfoundland.

The Tate Gallery

The Boyhood of Ralegh by J. E. Millais (1870)

"The Dawn and Rising Sun of Youth" . 5

His eyes followed them until they vanished one by one over the horizon. Then, reluctantly, he turned his back on the beach, scrambled up the red, rocky cliff, and trudged across the heathland toward his home.

The lure of the sea was in his blood. Six of the ships he had just watched belonged to his father. He had spent many an hour stolen from his lessons on the beaches of Devon, drinking in the tales of the seamen, tales of the fabulous lands beyond the rim of the horizon, tales that stirred his imagination so that he longed passionately to explore those lands for himself.

As the youngest son of an obscure country gentleman, Walter knew he had to make his own way in the world. Raleghs had lived in Devon for four hundred years. Once they had owned extensive lands, but the family had fallen on hard times. His father had been forced to give up his ancestral home, and gold was scarce in the thatched farmhouse manor of Hayes Barton where Walter had been born in 1554. The Raleghs were poor but they had their pride. His mother had relatives in high places at court and he had cousins among all the great families in the West of England.

Walter began to run. There was still a great deal to be done, and he had wasted the afternoon taking his last look at the sea and ships he loved. Tomorrow he must leave all that behind him, along with the woods where he had spent so many happy hours, the river Otter where he had gone fishing with his father, the high hills behind his home where he could climb and climb and feel himself on top of the world. His cousin Henry Champernowne was leading a band of gentleman volunteers to fight for the Huguenot cause in France's civil war, and Walter was to ride with him.

Once he had dreamed of going into battle at his half brother's side, but that had not been possible. Humphrey Gilbert, sixteen years older than he, had been his hero for as long as he could remember. At Humphrey's home on Dartmoor Walter had spent much of his childhood. There all the talk had been of the New World across the Atlantic. Tucked away in a corner of the candle-lit room smoky with great fires, Walter had listened to the captains who gathered there, fascinated by the tales they told of the Spanish treasure ships coming from Mexico and Peru with their cargoes of gold and silver, of jewels and fine satins, of spices and perfumes. To capture only one of them could make a poor man rich in a single voyage.

Humphrey had been educated at Eton and Oxford; he had been page to the queen when she was still a girl; he had fought in France; he had campaigned brilliantly in the Irish wars. He was not an easy-tempered man. His brown eyes would glow with enthusiasm for one of his own projects, but they could darken with anger if he were crossed.

With Walter he had always been wonderfully patient. He had taught him how to read a chart, how to take a bearing from the polestar, how to use an astrolabe, by which seamen measured the altitude of the sun and navigated their ships. Above all, he had opened up to the boy his own vision of carrying Elizabeth's kingdom to the Americas, of beating the Spaniards at their own game and founding an overseas empire that would make the name of England ring around the world. It was a dream to fire any lad with imagination and, in his father's opinion, Walter had far too much of that already.

That evening in the cozy living room with the great king-beam cut from a single oak spanning the ceiling, Walter knelt by the hearth, burnishing his sword and listening eagerly to the talk circulating around the table. Henry Champernowne had brought news of the court at Whitehall. London was nearly

"*The Dawn and Rising Sun of Youth*" : 7

three hundred miles away and reliable information traveled very slowly. It was a year since the country had buzzed with rumors about the Queen of Scotland's complicity in the murder of her husband, Lord Darnley. The case against her had never been proved, but she had married the Earl of Bothwell, who was undoubtedly one of his murderers, and all Scotland had risen against her. Now Mary had fled to England and Elizabeth had shut her up in Tutbury Castle.

"She is Catholic and subtle as a serpent for all her charm. She intrigues with Spain and the Pope," said Henry Champernowne gloomily. "She is likely to be a thorn in the side of our sovereign mistress for as long as she lives."

Walter's mother stood watching her youngest son. Barely fifteen, he was a good-looking boy, tall for his age, with dark hair curling above a high forehead. His face was pale, rather long and grave, the mouth full but firm, and the blue-gray eyes alive with an eager intelligence.

She was accustomed to sturdy sons; she had three from Otho Gilbert, her first husband—John, Humphrey, and Adrian—and there was Carew, Walter's older brother. But she feared for this last-born. Like the Gilberts, Walter was quick at learning, bursting with vitality and ambition. Sometimes she thought he might be going to outstrip them all, and yet she was anxious. He was too highly strung, too proud and sensitive and quick-tempered, too easily hurt and quick to resent it with a passionate anger that brought him punishment.

She sighed and thought how young he was to be going into battle, to see terrible wounds and death, and to learn of cruelty and injustice, all the hatefulness of men who fought so fiercely in the name of religion. But she knew she could not hold him back, and in the morning she saw him ride proudly away, with sword and lance and gleaming breastplate, and felt how empty the house would seem with only her elderly husband to keep her company.

The war in France was waged savagely and without pity. For years Protestant fought Catholic without mercy, honor, or chivalry on either side. It was to be a harsh, embittering experience for a boy of fifteen.

Walter set out on his first campaign with all the idealism of youth. He had grown up in the reformed faith. His father had been churchwarden of East Budleigh Church. Sunday after Sunday he had sat beside his parents directly under the preacher's eye, yawning through the two-hour sermon and amusing himself by letting his fingers trace the patterns on the finely carved pew ends—the Ralegh coat of arms held up by two stags, a ship in full sail, and a monstrous dragon—until his mother shook her head at him reprovingly. The rich language of the Bible, now read in English for the first time, was as familiar to him as his Latin grammar.

On October 3, 1569, he rode excitedly into battle at Montcontour under the grim black banner of a corpse with a severed head, with the motto *Let Valour End my life*. He experienced the shock and danger of defeat.

Champernowne's troops retreated to the south, where the Catholics had hidden themselves in the caves of Languedoc with their goods and their gold. There was only one entrance cut out in the high rocks and, not knowing how to enter except one by one, which would have been suicide, they let down bundles of burning straw. Walter thought it good fun until he saw the men come staggering out, choking, scorched by the flames, forced to surrender "or they must have died like bees that are smoked out of their hives."

The scene made him remember the burning of the heretics by the Catholic Mary Tudor, who had been Queen of England when he was still very young. In those dangerous times his father had nearly lost his life for his Protestant beliefs, and his mother had courageously visited a poor woman condemned to the stake for heresy at Exeter. She had come home deeply moved.

"If God were not with her, she could not speak such things," she had said. "I was not able to answer her—I who can read and she cannot."

Walter had never forgotten it.

As the days passed in France, Walter saw many terrible things: villages looted and burned, women tortured and babies slaughtered by his own soldiers as well as by the enemy. His young mind was confused. He began seeking after a wider, more universal belief, a God not shackled by rules and creeds for which men would ravage and murder and feel themselves in the right. All around him he heard wild talk, some of it blasphemous. There were those who said there was no God, no truth or honesty or idealism in the world. It was hard to hold on to the simple faith of his childhood.

"There are no such things as wars of religion," he was to write later, "only civil wars," and "by civil war no nation is ever bettered."

All his life he would fight to save men condemned simply for their faith, whether Catholic or Protestant, Puritan or heathen.

Walter's experiences in France toughened him both physically and mentally. His quick mind absorbed a great deal about the strategy of war and he learned how to endure hunger, thirst, fatigue, and sickness, as every soldier must. He was younger than his companions. They were a mixed bunch, mostly sons of noble families who were inclined to look down on Walter Ralegh, the poor boy from a humble country village. They mocked the Devonshire drawl in his speech, so he deepened it deliberately. He held himself aloof, remaining in his quarters reading while they caroused or gambled. He would always take delight in being different from those around him, so that he was called damnably proud and an arrogant young puppy.

After nearly three years of this murderous fighting, the war came to an end in an uneasy peace in April 1572, and the volunteers were no longer needed. As it turned out, the peace lasted only a few months. That summer on Saint Bartholomew's Day, Catherine de Medici, Queen Mother of France, fearful of the Huguenot influence on her son, Charles IX, incited the Catholics to fall upon the unsuspecting Protestants gathered in Paris for the marriage of their leader, Henri of Navarre, with the king's sister, Marguerite de Valois. The massacre shocked the English into a frenzied hatred of all Catholics. The unhappy French ambassador, summoned before the queen to give an explanation of the tragedy, found Elizabeth with her ladies and her privy councilors dressed in somber black and could only stammer out a few helpless words.

But by this time Walter was back in England, a soldier no longer, but a scholar on his way to Oriel College, Oxford. As he jogged peacefully along the narrow lanes, the countryside seemed green and untouched after the devastation of France. Instead of burning ricks and ruined hovels, Walter saw fat cattle grazing in the rich meadows, flocks of sheep, ripening wheat and barley, and well-fed country folk going contentedly about their work in the fields.

Walter was eighteen, two years older than most of the students going up to the university, and he still was not sure what

The New York Public Library Picture Collection

Queen Elizabeth and her court, dressed in mourning, receive the French ambassadors after the news of the Massacre of St. Bartholomew

he wanted to make of his life. Soldier . . . sailor . . . either had a great appeal for him. He had missed the sea while he was in France. It was during those years that Francis Drake, another Devonshire man, had sailed to Africa and South America with his uncle, the great merchant seaman John Hawkins. They had fought the Spaniards heroically in the harbor of San Juan de Uloa and Drake had escaped, sailing his tiny ship *Judith* all the way home. Now he was planning a new voyage to Panama, where the Spaniards loaded their ships with silver from Peru. Walter was filled with envy.

But these thoughts were in the back of Walter's mind as he rode into Oxford. He paused on Folly Bridge to look downstream where the Thames flowed away to London. The splendor of the city's many stone spires stretched before him. He passed up St. Aldate's, the magnificence of Cardinal Wolsey's great college of Christ Church on his right, and found Oriel at last, where he was directed to a room off the ancient quadrangle that he would share with four other students.

The college Fellow who would be their tutor immediately read them an impressive list of rules. Walter did not even trouble to listen. He was not a schoolboy. The years in France had given him a tough outer shell of independence, even of aggressiveness. In no time he was making his mark in the life of the university.

The students were always staging debates. In the college halls they would argue on every subject imaginable and Walter, starved of mental activity in France, plunged joyously into the debates, discovering a power of wit and sharp repartee that did not make him popular but that won him respect. He did, however, make a few good friends, whom he would keep close to him all through his stormy life.

"The Dawn and Rising Sun of Youth" : 13

Arthur Gorges was a second cousin from Somerset, a dashing young gallant with a keen wit and an eye for a pretty girl, but they had much in common. They both loved learning and had a passionate interest in poetry. They would dash off verses about anything and everything, passing them around among their friends and acquaintances.

Then there was George Carew, another cousin, from Devonshire, a quiet, very serious young man, at first a little doubtful of his wild young relative. But, for those he liked, Walter was always to possess an irresistible charm.

"These West Countrymen stick together like burrs," grumbled Master Child, one of his roommates, very annoyed because Walter, always in a hurry to join his cousins, had borrowed his gown and failed to return it.

He was reading logic, rhetoric, and philosophy and had begun to find the teaching old-fashioned and cramping to his keen intelligence. Some of the most brilliant students at Oxford were Catholic and left early to go to Louvain or Rheims, where they could practice their religion in peace. Many of the tutors were strict Puritans.

"Your loose gown becomes you better than your narrow notions," Queen Elizabeth had remarked dryly to old Dr. Humphreys, the president of Magdalen College, when he bent to kiss her hand. Walter would have agreed with her. He found that a freely inquiring intellect always hunting after new ideas was severely frowned on. So far as science, mathematics, and geography were concerned, Oxford was still stuck fast in the Dark Ages.

Still, there were compensations. There were no athletics, no organized games, but the students went swimming in the river Isis. They fished; they played tennis. They fenced and practiced with bow and arrow. They diced and gambled in the taverns, all strictly forbidden by the authorities, but that did not trouble Walter or his friends.

In the college halls plays, interludes, and masques were presented in Latin, which the boys had been taught to read and speak since childhood. It was a kind of universal language among the educated classes of all European countries. A German traveler visiting England who had unfortunately lost his way in the wilds of Oxfordshire wrote thankfully in his diary: "A gentleman asked us in Latin where we wanted to get to and left his wife and ladies to show us the right way. . . . That day I would not have missed knowing Latin for a thaler."

But most important to Walter was his friendship with Richard Hakluyt. Hakluyt was studying theology at Christ Church, but his great ambition was to compile a book of all the English voyages of discovery from the earliest times. Walter neglected his tutor to spend hours with him, his imagination stirred by the accounts he was helping to decipher, often in the crabbed handwriting of sea captains and sailors. It was fascinating to try and sift fact from legend. Cortes had conquered Mexico, Pizarro had discovered the Inca Empire of Peru and now the gold poured into Spain. On the ancient, clumsily drawn charts Walter's eye traced the great stretch of North America from Newfoundland to Florida, still largely unmapped and unexplored, wide open to any adventurous spirit.

2 : "Fortune, my Foe"

—Walter Ralegh

In 1575 Walter left the university without taking a degree and, like every poor young man, headed for London to seek fame and fortune. Poverty had forced his parents to give up Hayes and move to a small house his father owned in the cathedral close at Exeter. One day, Walter vowed, he would buy back the reed-thatched farmhouse where he had played as a baby and dreamed his boyish dreams of an empire beyond the Atlantic. But first he had to win his own place in the world.

He rode into the city on the Oxford Road past the great gibbets of Tyburn where thieves and murderers were strung up as a public spectacle. He followed the banks of the Tyburn stream to where it flowed into the Thames. The magnificent abbey church of Westminster was on his right, and beyond lay St. Stephen's Chapel, where the members of Parliament met, and the medieval hall built in 1309 where traitors had stood trial for more than two hundred years.

He glanced at them with admiration but was far more interested in the palace of Whitehall sprawling along the river bank. It had been so enlarged and rebuilt since Henry VIII had snatched it from Cardinal Wolsey that it lay in a great jumble of turrets, halls, and red roofs, with a road running through it, spanned by two bridges at either end. On the left were tennis courts, a badminton court, a bowling green, a cockpit, and the tiltyard, while beyond was the grass of St. James's Park, with a huge lake where swans and cranes nested and the deer came down to feed at the waterside.

The palace hummed with a busy throng of messengers, officials in long dark gowns, soldiers in the uniform of the Queen's Guard, and brilliantly dressed courtiers with their retinues, all going in and out before his fascinated eyes.

Reluctantly, he left it behind and rode on through the open fields, past the houses of the great nobles with their gardens going down to the Thames, until he reached the Temple Gate and the entrance to the city itself.

"It is a very populous city so that one can scarcely pass along the streets on account of the throng," wrote a distinguished foreign visitor. "The inhabitants are magnificently appareled and are extremely proud and overbearing; and because the greater part . . . seldom go into other countries . . . they care little for foreigners, but scoff and laugh at them; and moreover one dare not oppose them, else the streetboys and apprentices collect together in immense crowds and strike to right and left unmercifully without regard to person."

The citizens were notorious for their rough and rude behavior. So Walter found as he forced his horse forward, buffeted by the casks carried on the backs of the saucy water-carriers and thrust aside by the insolent servingmen of the great lords. His ears were deafened by the sound of bells ringing out from the many churches for a service, a funeral, a wedding, or just because the exuberant Londoners enjoyed making a great noise.

Presently the reek from the Fleet Ditch and the open sewers running along the streets drove him down to the river, where the air was fresher. He paused near the bridge, impressed by the twenty great arches spanning the Thames and the road running across between the tall gabled houses. Above rose the huge stakes that held the heads of traitors pecked white to the bone by the hordes of kites swooping down to feast on the piles of garbage in the gutters.

He glanced at the massive stronghold of the Tower but looked with a great deal more interest at the host of shipping in the Pool of London. Merchantmen from France, Denmark, the Netherlands, Germany, even from Venice and Portugal, crowded together with the queen's fighting ships, while up and down the boatmen plied for hire. They were an independent body of men, and when a passenger went down the steps to the waterside and shouted "Oars!" they would bring up their wherries, look him up and down, and demand to see the color of his money before rowing him to his destination.

Humphrey Gilbert was living at Limehouse, just beyond the city limits. From the windows of the study Walter could look downstream to the shipbuilding yards of Peter Pett at Deptford and the queen's palace at Greenwich

"Register at one of the Inns of Court," advised his half brother when they talked together after supper. "A knowledge of the law is always useful."

So Walter enrolled as a student of the Middle Temple in February 1575, though he had no intention of studying seriously for a legal career. The Inns of Court—Lincoln's Inn, Gray's Inn, Lyon Inn, and the Temple—were like a London university for all the young blades of the town, all the gentlemanly younger sons who haunted the court in the hope of persuading someone of influence to recommend them for a good post.

It was a more mature society than at Oxford. Walter found it intoxicating to take part in the literary disputes and soon won a reputation for ironic wit and a sarcastic turn of humor.

The plays and masques staged by the Inns of Court were famous. In 1562 they had presented before the Queen's Majesty at Whitehall *Gorboduc* or *Ferrex and Porrex*, remarkable because it was the first tragedy to be written in English instead of Latin, and on that evening dashing young Christopher Hatton had danced his way into Elizabeth's heart. Now he held the coveted post of Captain of her Guard. It went to show how much could be gained if only the queen smiled on one.

Roger Ascham, who had been tutor to Elizabeth in her girlhood, once drew up a list of a young gentleman's accomplishments: "To ride comely; to run fair at Tilt or ring; to play at all weapons; to shoot fair in bow or surely in gun; to dance comely; to sing and play of instruments cunningly; to hawk; to hunt; to play at tennis."

All of them were individual talents. This was an age of individualism, and the team spirit was unknown.

Walter took part in all these pastimes. One part of him enjoyed the turbulent life of the students, the mad frolics, and the jests they played on one another, and he had a short sharp way with those who bored him. One evening in a tavern where "a bold impertinent fellow and perpetual talker" interrupted their conversation with his "noise like a drum," Walter leaped upon the unfortunate man, sealing his beard to his mustache with hard wax and effectively silencing him for the next hour or two.

But he had other more serious occupations. He had found himself lodgings at Islington, a little country village to the north of the city, where he could walk by the river and go duck shooting in the woody marshes. There he would read French and Italian, and he would study books on military strategy and navigation and the movements of the stars. Sometimes, when the fancy took him, he would write poetry.

He was leading a hand-to-mouth existence on the little his father could allow him, for Humphrey was very nearly as poor as himself. With all his brilliance, Walter's half brother had not been fortunate. He had been knighted for his services in France and Ireland, but back pay was still owing to him, and he wrote beseeching letters to the Privy Council lamenting that he was being forced to sell the clothes off his wife's back in order to eat.

Humphrey still dreamed of America and the colony he was going to establish there. He was putting the finishing touches to a pamphlet intended to persuade the queen that there was a Northwest Passage through the Arctic Ocean to India and the fabled riches of the East, which could be found if only she would grant him a charter and ships to explore it. Unfortunately it was a dream that, like a will-o'-the-wisp, was to lure many seamen to their deaths before they realized its impossibility.

The pamphlet was to be published by George Gascoigne, a swashbuckling adventurer who was also a soldier, a Cambridge scholar, and a poet, tossing off verses, translations, short stories, and playlets by the dozen. He was in high favor because of the brilliant entertainment he had devised for his patron, the great Earl of Leicester, when the queen visited the earl's castle of Kenilworth that summer. It was Walter's luck to meet him, for he not only did Walter the honor of selecting one of his poems to print with his own satire, *The Steel Glass*, but promised to do his best to introduce him into the court.

He kept his promise. At twenty-three Walter was duly sworn in as an Esquire of the Body, one of a great number of very minor young gentlemen from whom the queen, or her council, might recruit someone to carry a dispatch, travel with an ambassador's retinue, or attend her on one of her many progresses.

Restless and ambitious, Walter soon found his duties more tedious than exacting. He was burning to attract the queen's notice but was given no opportunity. Standing in the Presence Chamber among a great many other young men, he would watch from afar the woman on whom all attention was fixed, who was the source of all favor. His eyes followed enviously those who went with her into the intimacy of her Privy Chamber.

There was the Earl of Leicester, her "dear Robin," the one man whom she had loved and might have married if she had not dedicated herself to the rule of her kingdom. Robert Dudley was a magnificent figure still, though his handsome face was beginning to show the lines of too much good living. He had acknowledged Walter's existence with a careless nod when Gascoigne presented him.

Then there was William Cecil, Lord Burghley, her treasurer and most trusted councilor, with his grave air and long gray beard. Elizabeth had nicknames for all those close to her. Burghley was her "Spirit," and the dark, astute Sir Francis Walsingham, the Secretary of State, was her "Moor." Leicester was her "Eyes," and Christopher Hatton she called her "Lids" and sometimes her "Sheep"—and sheeplike he was too, thought Walter scornfully, with his sweet smile and waving chestnut hair.

"Fortune, my Foe" : 21

But it was Elizabeth herself who occupied Walter's thoughts and gripped his imagination. Gloriana her people called her, or Diana, virgin huntress and Goddess of the Moon. She was forty-five, but she seemed ageless, her face ivory pale with eyes golden to green, delicately arched eyebrows, high-bridged aquiline nose.

"I was never beautiful," she admitted once, "though in my youth I had the reputation of it."

She had more than beauty, he thought. She was Cynthia, Lady of the Sea. Already he was writing verses to her in his mind:

To serve, to live, to look upon those eyes,
To look, to live, to kiss that heavenly hand.

Her subjects were dazzled by the pale satin gowns shimmering with gold and silver, by the gauze ruffs like transparent wings framing the red-gold hair gleaming with jewels above the high forehead. Even foreign ambassadors with no cause to flatter wrote home ecstatically of her brilliant mind and her witty conversation, and rather ruefully of her devilish cleverness.

At this time she was pretending to consider a project of marriage with the French king's brother, the Duc d'Alençon, a young man so small and ugly with his pockmarked face that she called him her "Frog."

"What compensation do I get in the marriage articles for his enormous nose?" she asked her council jestingly.

She would pass through the Presence Chamber laughing with her intimate friends, pausing now and again to single out some fortunate young man for her attention, but she never once looked in Walter's direction, or if she did, he was not aware of it.

One day in the spring of 1578 he saw her in the gardens of

National Portrait Gallery

Elizabeth I

Leicester's country house at Wanstead in a white dress embroidered with sprays of flowers, smiling graciously at Sir Philip Sidney and giving him a lock of her hair as he knelt at her feet rapturously speaking his gratitude.

> Like sparkling gems, her virtue draws the sight
> And in her conduct she is always bright.
> When she imparts her thoughts, her words have force
> And sense and wisdom flow in sweet discourse.

Walter, so conscious of his own gifts and certain of his own abilities, still envied the young man so favored. Sidney was Leicester's nephew, the same age as Walter, good-looking, a poet with infinite charm, the ideal young courtier. How lucky it was to have fortune on your side.

Walter's own pockets were even emptier than usual. Once during the past two years he had slipped away and joined one of the bands of English volunteers fighting for the Protestant cause against the Spanish in the Netherlands, but it had led to nothing. He had returned poorer than he set out. Now it was only a few months since his two young servants who had come up to him from Devon had been hauled before the city magistrate for rioting in the streets. He had been forced to find the money somehow to pay their heavy fine. Adrian Gilbert had come to his rescue with a loan of £60, but the Lord only knew when he would be able to repay it.

Then quite suddenly everything changed. He returned to London in June to find Humphrey on fire with enthusiasm. He had been granted a charter authorizing him to search for and occupy with English settlers lands "not actually possessed of any Christian prince or people."

All the previous summer in the study at Limehouse they had been poring over the latest maps and charters. Sometimes they would be joined by Martin Frobisher, a big clumsy man who spoke with a broad Yorkshire accent. He had no learning, but he was a brilliant navigator who had already voyaged to the East and searched for that elusive Northwest Passage to Cathay. He had returned from his last trip, his ships stuffed with black ore that he was certain contained gold. Unluckily, it proved a false hope, and the people jeered at him for a credulous fool.

Now the queen had at last yielded to Humphrey's pleading and had promised to loan one of her own ships, the *Falcon*, a naval vessel of a hundred tons.

"And you are to be her captain, Wat, my boy," said Humphrey cheerfully, clapping his brother on the shoulder.

So she must have taken notice of him after all. Elizabeth would never have trusted one of her precious ships to him otherwise. A feeling of elation ran through him. It was his first chance to show her what he could do.

The summer months raced by all too quickly while they tried to raise sufficient hard cash to fit out the ships and make them ready for sea. There were plenty of young men eager to join the expedition, but the rich city merchants were unwilling to invest their gold without a certainty of profit. Humphrey's plans, which included orders "to seize upon and hinder the Spanish trade in the West Indies," had to be kept secret, since the Spanish ambassador was already clamoring for the voyage to be stopped.

Officially England was at peace with Spain, but that did not prevent English seamen from capturing and plundering every Spanish treasure ship they came across on the high seas. Francis Drake, "El Draque" as he was called by the Spaniards, the fearful dragon with whom Spanish mothers frightened their babies when they were naughty, had been looting Spanish settlements in the New World, and Elizabeth turned a blind eye to it. She demanded her share of the plunder when it was brought back to England. At the very same time she was writing regretful letters to King Philip in Madrid swearing that she knew nothing about such piratical ventures, and as soon as she captured the culprits they would be severely punished.

Walter was proud of his first command. The *Falcon*, with a crew of seventy, was the fourth largest ship in the fleet of eleven. His master, who would sail the ship, was an experienced Portuguese seaman called Ferdinando, but it was never Walter's way to order men to do what he could not do himself. George Carew, who was sailing with him, smiled at his determination to master every detail down to the last load of beef, ale, and ship's biscuit that was carried aboard.

By autumn sufficient money had been raised, mostly from friends and relatives in Devon. Down in Plymouth on a fine frosty day Walter accompanied Humphrey and the other captains, with as many of the men as could be spared, to morning service at St. Andrew's Church to pray for the success of the voyage. Then they hurried down to their ships to sail with the afternoon tide.

The expedition met with bad luck from the start. Southwesterly gales from the Azores buffeted and tore at their sails, forcing them back into harbor. Henry Knollys, who was second in command, a proud, overbearing man, quarreled violently with the hot-tempered Humphrey. He swung off on his own, turning pirate and hunting for ships he could capture and loot for himself.

Humphrey seized a cargo of oranges and lemons from a Seville merchantman in the English Channel, was ordered to return it, and refused. He believed, ahead of his time, that the fresh fruit helped to combat scurvy, the terrible disease that killed so many seamen on long voyages where the only food was salted meat and hard biscuit.

The ships set out again in the teeth of winter storms, but one by one they became separated and struggled back to port. Only Walter sailed on alone, taking his course for the West Indies, since now it was too late in the year to venture into the icy waters around Newfoundland and explore the coast for the future colony. He was determined not to give up without winning glory for the queen.

He never reached his destination. Spanish ships had been alerted against him. Off Cape Verde he met their attack for the first time. It was a desperate struggle. The *Falcon* was the queen's ship. To surrender was unthinkable. No English ship had ever yielded to the enemy, and if he was captured, it would mean years in a Spanish prison, torture by the Inquisition, the end of all his ambitions. He fought on relentlessly.

To the ship's boys running between magazine and guns, their hands filled with powder and shot, the lower deck seemed like a scene out of hell. The men stripped to the waist were streaming with sweat in the burning heat and everything was lit by the lurid red glow of the gun flashes. Faces were blackened by smoke, throats clogged with the bitter smell of the spilled gunpowder. The metal barrels were so hot they seared the fingers. The water sizzled and spat as buckets were emptied over the guns to cool them. Every now and again a shot reached its mark, the wounded were dragged away, and a fresh gun crew took their place.

On the upper deck slippery with water and blood, Walter narrowly escaped death from a sharpshooter high in the rigging of a Spanish galleon, but wounded though he was, he still fought on. By nightfall they were battered, but they were afloat, and it was the enemy who crept away in the darkness.

The battle destroyed any chance of exploring further. He dared not sail on with half his crew dead or disabled by wounds. Their food was running short and water had to be strictly rationed. Sick with fever, he needed all his skill to bring the ship safely back home.

The *Falcon* limped into Plymouth in May 1579, and immediately Walter was involved in trouble. Humphrey was charging Knollys with desertion and Knollys was second cousin to the queen. The question of the oranges was thrashed out, their value against scurvy dismissed as an idle fancy, and the fine imposed was a large one. The council summoned the brothers to give an account of their voyage and sternly forbade any further attempts. There was nothing to be done but return to the idle, useless life at court which Walter had grown to despise but which at least made him sure of two good meals a day and some sort of a bed.

All that summer Whitehall buzzed with excitement. Simier, the dark little Frenchman whom the queen called her "Monkey," had come to woo on behalf of his master, the Duc d'Alençon. Slyly he revealed to Elizabeth his discovery of the secret marriage between the Earl of Leicester and the widowed Countess of Essex and smiled to himself at the rumpus he had created.

The queen was filled with rage. That her dear Robin who had declared himself her devoted admirer for thirty years should marry without her consent or knowledge was more than could be endured. He was thrown into prison. The Lord Chamberlain begged for his pardon, and Leicester was released but banished to his home at Wanstead. He promptly took to his bed—so ill that he was reported dying of grief—until the queen rushed to his bedside and stayed there for two whole days while he persuaded her to forgive, if not to forget.

By the end of the year Leicester was back in favor, and Walter saw the New Year gift he made to Elizabeth, a splendid set of gold buttons decorated with diamonds and rubies in truelove knots. He had never felt his poverty so keenly.

Walter had enjoyed his first experience of command and longed for action in which he could prove his worth. Frustrated and irritable, he rashly quarreled with Thomas Perrot, a young courtier whose father was Sir John Perrot, a notable soldier and an illegitimate son of Henry VIII and fond of boasting of his relationship to the queen.

Public quarrels were not encouraged at the royal court. Both young men were reprimanded and clapped into the Fleet prison for a week to cool their hot tempers: not a very severe punishment but galling to Walter's proud and rebellious spirit. A month later, after promises of good behavior, he was in trouble again.

Altogether young Walter Ralegh was behaving far too recklessly, thought Lord Burghley, signing a warrant for yet another week's imprisonment, this time for picking up his sword and threatening his opponent on the tennis court of all places. What could be done with such a fiery spirit?

Walter had even quarreled with the Earl of Oxford—not that the Lord Treasurer blamed him very much for that. The brilliant and unstable young nobleman was Burghley's son-in-law and had recently called Philip Sidney an insolent young puppy in front of the whole court. Only the queen's intervention had prevented a duel between them. Now Ralegh's name had been added to what Oxford called his "murder" list.

These young men! Burghley sighed and thanked heaven for his own second son. Robert Cecil was such a nice quiet boy, so good at his studies, the apple of his father's eye.

In the meantime, there was Walter Ralegh to be dealt with. He was a great deal too independent, too outspoken, too ready to criticize. The Lord Treasurer was conservative and disliked too many new ideas. However, Sir Francis Walsingham had been inclined to think the young man showed promise, Leicester had spoken of him, even the Queen's Majesty had deigned to mention him as someone to be watched.

He turned over letters from Lord Grey, the new Deputy in Ireland. Rebellion had broken out again and Grey was demanding more troops. It was just what was needed. A year or two fighting the savage Irish should be enough to keep any young man out of trouble.

On July 11, 1580, when he was twenty-six, Walter received a commission as captain of a company of footmen, together with £100 for expenses, and was ordered to embark from Portsmouth with all possible speed.

3 : *"I live to serve"*

—Walter Ralegh

"Ireland is a terrible country," warned Humphrey when the brothers supped together before Walter rode down to Portsmouth. "The native-born peasants are slippery as serpents. They wrap themselves in enormous yellow shirts and never take them off again till they're worn to rags. Their hair hangs in a shaggy mat over their eyes so that you can't tell whether they're true men or a pack of liars and they sleep all huddled together—men, women, and children—in hovels we wouldn't keep our pigs in. Above all, don't put your trust in the Earl of Ormonde. His family have owned land there since the Norman Conquest. He is hand in glove with the rebels."

Ormonde was cousin to the queen and was Lord General of Munster. There seemed a great distance between him and the insignificant Captain Ralegh with his hundred pikemen.

Walter's first base was Cork. He arrived after a wretched sea trip of seventeen days and energetically set about drilling his little band. Conditions were even more horrible than Humphrey had foretold. His living quarters were disgustingly dirty and the food almost uneatable—hard oatcake and meat served half raw without salt or sauce. Even the butter was streaked with hair from the cowshed and the superstitious Irish considered it unlucky to scour out the milk pails. There was no ale or wine to drink, nothing but a raw spirit distilled by the natives that they called usquebaugh or whiskey. Walter disliked it intensely.

The war was as ruthless and as murderous as it had been in France. The Irish came out of the woods at night "like hags and furies of hell with flakes of fire fastened on poles' ends," burning the thatched houses in villages and towns, then vanishing again like smoke into their bogs. Walter said once that to fight them was to "fight as one beating the air."

There was little mercy shown on either side. George Carew's elder brother was stripped of his armor and brutally slain when his horse was killed under him. The families of some of the English soldiers left behind in the villages were cruelly murdered. News came through that Spain had sent reinforcements to aid the rebels and win Ireland away from the heretic Queen Elizabeth and back into the Catholic Church. It inflamed the English to madness. Lord Grey, a stern Puritan, attacked the invaders mercilessly in the fort of Smerwick, where they had entrenched themselves, and, when they surrendered, ordered the garrison to be pitilessly slaughtered.

A few weeks later Walter, marching to join Lord Grey, came upon a small band of Irish peasants creeping through the deserted camp hunting for plunder. One of them came into the open, carrying on his shoulder the long branches of willow they had been cutting in the marsh. Confronted with the English captain, he threw down his bundle and would have ducked away, but the soldiers were too quick for him. Walter looked at him twisting and writhing in their hands and kicked at the bundle of branches at his feet.

"What is the use of these?" he asked.

"To hang up English churls," the rebel spat back at him.

"Is that so?" Without warning, a black rage boiled up in Walter. "Then they shall serve to hang up an Irish peasant," he snapped. It was not until the miserable wretch was swinging from a tree that he knew he could not kill the others, not out of pity but in a kind of disgust at himself. He allowed the rest of the peasants to flee.

Though officially under Lord Grey's command, Walter and his small band fought a brilliant little guerrilla war of their own during the next few months. They scoured the countryside, seeming to travel by lightning, turning up unexpectedly, wiping out pockets of rebels and melting away again into the bogs and forests, scarcely losing a man. Walter's daredevil courage and gallantry won the devotion of his soldiers. He did what he could to secure food and weapons for them, and they followed him loyally, with a firm belief in his ability and his luck.

Despite his successes, Walter was unpopular with his commander-in-chief. Lord Grey was a handsome and distinguished man, a patron of the arts, an able leader, but strict in his views and jealous of his reputation. He took an instant dislike to this young man from Devonshire who was impertinent enough to stand up at the council table and openly criticize the way in which he was waging the war. The dispatches sent to London contained no mention of Captain Ralegh's exploits, but all the same his daring and ability had not gone entirely unnoticed. He was granted a troop of horsemen in addition to his little band of infantry and given a new commission to bring back to Cork a certain Lord Roche, suspected of aiding the Irish.

Walter collected his orders from Lord Ormonde and, as he hurried to rejoin his troop, took a short cut across enemy country. He was riding well ahead of his four companions when he heard galloping hoofs behind him, and a glance over his shoulder caused him to regret his rashness. The chieftain of Imokilly, with whom he had often skirmished, had caught him in a trap. He was cut off from his men and only the river Blackwater lay ahead; he put spurs to his horse and raced on.

The Blackwater was flowing perilously fast, but he plunged in and with difficulty scrambled up the farther bank. The Irishmen pulled up, for their rough ponies drew back from the flooding water. They moved up the strand to find an easier crossing.

One of Walter's men riding not far behind his captain reached the river and also took the plunge, but his horse reared so high he was thrown backward into the current. Walter heard his despairing shrieks for help. The chieftain was still watching, but at the risk of his own life, Walter coaxed his own reluctant horse back into the torrent. The raging water beat against him as he leaned over to get a grip on the drowning man's belt. Walter dragged him ashore and, while he choked and spat, stood with his pistol in one hand and his quarterstaff in the other, guarding him and the other three men as they came up and forded their way across the river.

The big Irishman with his band of twenty stood motionless. Why he did not attack, Walter never knew. Maybe he saw his own death in the frowning eyes of the young man grimly watching his every movement.

Reunited with his troop, Walter was faced with the certainty that Lord Roche could summon five hundred well-armed followers to oppose him, and his own ninety would not be of much avail against such odds. He quietly placed them as near the castle as possible. Then, using all his considerable charm and persuasion, he obtained admittance on the plea of urgent business with Lord Roche.

Lord Roche could hardly refuse hospitality to a fellow countryman. After dinner, Walter produced his commission.

"I am sorry, my lord," he said courteously, "but I am under strict orders to conduct you and your lady back with me to Cork."

"And if I refuse to obey?" was the haughty reply.

"If you will not come willingly, then I regret to say that it must be unwillingly," said Walter quietly.

There was a breathless moment of suspense. It would have been easy for Lord Roche to have Walter and his few comrades killed long before his soldiers could reach them, except that if he did so, he would draw down on himself the hatred and disgust of all other Englishmen. Looking into the steady eyes of the young man who stood with such confidence, one hand lightly on his sword hilt, Lord Roche knew he was defeated and yielded with bad grace.

Walter brought his prisoners safely to Cork through a black night of storm and rain. He had lost only one man in the action, but he got no thanks for it, and there was a foolish repercussion from his skirmish with the chief of Imokilly.

The Irishman had sought a parley with the Earl of Ormonde and took the opportunity to speak contemptuously of Captain Ralegh, boasting of his generosity in sparing his life. The insult in front of his brother officers was more than Walter's pride could endure, and he replied with taunts of cowardice.

Ormonde listened, half smiling, looking from one to the other, one hand caressing his scented, well-trimmed beard.

He said coolly, "It is easy enough settled. Take your four men to the riverbank and challenge the chief to fight it out, Ralegh. I am sure he would be delighted to oblige."

"With all my heart, my lord."

At that moment Walter would willingly have fought the whole band single-handed, but the rebel leader was not to be tempted. He refused the challenge with contempt.

Walter fretted out the summer months, chafing against the restrictions that kept him in a subordinate position. He was too clever, too independent; he argued too hotly with his superiors over the orders he was forced to carry out.

"I have spent some time here under the deputy in such poor place and charge as were it not for that I know him to be one of yours I would disdain it as much as to keep sheep," he wrote to Lord Leicester and followed it up with even more scathing criticism of the Earl of Ormonde, under whose rule, he pointed out, "there are at this instant a thousand traitors more than there were the first day."

No sensible man would have spoken so recklessly of the queen's dear cousin, but Walter never remembered to guard what he wrote. His rash pen ran on in passionate pleading for Humphrey, who Walter thought had never received the praise or reward due to him. "Would to God the service of Sir Humphrey Gilbert might be rightly looked into: who, with the third part of the garrison now in Ireland, ended a rebellion not much inferior to this, in two months."

It did him no good with Lord Grey, and that autumn he nearly lost his life pitting his small force against far greater numbers. Once, when his horse was killed under him, only the swift action of one of his loyal soldiers saved him from death.

Back in Dublin, he reaped the bitter reward of his own criticism. He was sent back to England with dispatches that contained no word of his own brilliant service. "For my own part," wrote Lord Grey icily, "I must be plain. I like neither his carriage nor his company."

So there he was, back in London, twenty-eight now, still almost as penniless as when he left Oxford, and saddened by the news that his father had died while he was away.

Life at the Palace of Whitehall was brilliant compared to the desolation of Ireland. The court was deep in the business of preparing for the Christmas festivities.

Some months before, Drake had returned from his three-year voyage around the world, bringing Elizabeth gold and silver and jewels worth more than a million pounds. All of England went wild about him. Even the children in the nursery were singing a new rhyme about him:

> I saw a ship a-sailing,
> A-sailing on the sea,
> And oh! it was all laden,
> With pretty things for thee!
>
> There were comfits in the cabin,
> And apples in the hold,
> The sails were made of silk,
> And the masts were made of gold.

Mendoza, the Spanish ambassador, had demanded the pirate's death for the damage he had inflicted on Spain's possessions in the Pacific, but the queen refused to listen or even to see him. "She is possessed by ten thousand devils," he wrote in a fury to his king.

She smiled graciously as she accepted the tiny frog made from the looted diamonds that Drake had ordered a London jeweler

Queen Elizabeth Knighting Sir Francis Drake by John Gilbert

to create for her. "I have come to cut off your head," she said gaily when she lifted the sword and knighted him on the deck of the *Golden Hind*.

Walter saw the ship lying in the Thames at Deptford, one of the sights of London that everyone had flocked to visit during the summer.

He had delivered his official letters and waited in vain all through the dark days of December. He was still only on the fringe of the court, one of its most insignificant members, but it was now, at the lowest ebb of his fortunes, when the future had never seemed more gloomy, that the great adventure of his life was about to begin.

A contemporary was to write: "But true it is he had gotten the queen's ear in a trice, and she began to be taken with his elocution and loved to hear his reasons to her demands; and the truth is, she took him for a kind of oracle, which nettled them all."

Walter had been summoned before the council to give an account of his service in Ireland and to answer questions about the ideas he had so freely expressed in his daringly outspoken letters. They were all there in the great room with its richly paneled walls and magnificently gilded ceiling—Burghley, Walsingham, Leicester, and the queen herself in white and silver, diamonds glittering in her hair and in the handle of the scarlet-feather fan with which her beautiful hands were toying.

Elizabeth watched him as he approached the table. She saw a tall, very lean young man, unquestionably good-looking, with the forehead of an intellectual and rich dark hair that curled naturally, like the small, well-trimmed beard. She noted with approval the long fine hands, the elegance of his dress, on which he had recklessly spent far more than he could afford. There was a charm about this young man. He was so intensely alive.

She was captivated by his boldness, by the ease and clarity with which he expressed himself, even by the Devon drawl that he made no attempt to conceal. He had a vitality lacking in her precise courtiers. He interested and intrigued her. But the queen had always been a shrewd judge of character. There was more to him than a handsome face and she recognized his quality.

Some time during the days that followed, there came the moment he had been waiting for all his life. One afternoon when she came through the Presence Chamber, she paused, looked across at him, and beckoned him to her side.

All around there were surprised and hostile glances, but he did not care. Daringly he looked into the green eyes of the unpredictable woman who had fascinated him from the first day he had seen her. This was his destiny and he rushed to meet it, disregarding danger and careless of what it might bring.

> Whoso wins renown above the rest
> With heaps of hate shall surely be oppressed.

He had written these words in an early poem and never realized how true it was to prove of his own life.

4 : *"Dear Empress of my Heart"*

—Walter Ralegh

Elizabeth's "Frog" prince was going back to France. For three years she had played with the idea of marriage, changing her mind from day to day, arguing with Burghley, with Leicester, with Walsingham, even with Philip Sidney, all hotly against a French match for their queen. But she knew very well what she was doing. In the twenty-five years of her reign she had raised her small island kingdom to a place of importance in Europe, and it had not been easy. The two great powers, France and Spain, were Catholic, and England was Protestant. She had to keep the balance between them. She had to keep her country safe and free from the threat of war and she had done it by convincing the French prince that she was in earnest, by playing off one great country against the other.

Now the danger was over for the moment and she accompanied the prince as far as Canterbury, making quite sure that his journey home included a visit to the naval dockyards at Chatham. They presented an impressive spectacle that took the Frenchman's breath away.

"Well might the nations call Queen Elizabeth the Queen of the Sea!" he exclaimed at sight of the newly completed ships crowding the quays. In the yards, vessels were being built of unusual and improved design that was to prove its worth in time to come.

She bade him a tearful farewell, saying that she would not live until her "Frog" came swimming back again up the Thames, but her maids of honor whispered that in the privacy of her bedroom she was dancing with joy that the long ordeal was over.

The prince embarked at the end of February 1582, escorted by Leicester and a hundred gentlemen, among whom was Walter, magnificently equipped and entrusted by the queen with a special confidential mission to William of Orange in the Netherlands. He came back in March and within a few weeks had been drawn into the innermost circle of those around the queen.

It was the rapidity of his rise to favor that caused so much envy and jealousy. From nothing he was suddenly closer to Elizabeth than anyone. It was as if two brilliantly clever people were discovering one another for the first time, and it seemed as if she would never tire of his company nor he of hers. He must be constantly by her side, hunting with her at Windsor, riding with her at Hampton Court, talking to her in the evenings at Whitehall, when after she had supped, she would call her young courtiers around her and the conversation would range over a dozen different topics.

Elizabeth had always liked the men about her to be good-looking. She took pleasure in Walter's tall figure, the graceful carriage, the unusual eyes, sometimes blue as a summer sea and sometimes darkening to a somber gray. As Burghley was her "Spirit" and Leicester her "Eyes," so he became "Water," both a play on his name and a reminder of his variable moods.

He could talk to her in French and Italian. His Latin was good and he could translate Spanish for her. He had read widely. He could discuss poetry, religion, history, or philosophy with equal ease. He could be witty and amusing and no one else had written her such verses. Riding high in her favor, he felt the words flashing through his mind like fireflies. He had to write them down.

> Those eyes that set my fancy on a fire,
> That wit which of my thoughts doth hold the reins . . .

or

> Time wears her not; she doth his Chariot guide,
> Mortality below her orb is placed.

Every day a new poem was dropped in her lap. Elizabeth was nearly fifty. It flattered and pleased her that she could charm this fascinating young soldier twenty years younger than herself. He was the first man to stir her heart since her stormy passion for Leicester, but that was long ago when she was young, and now her "dear Robin" was married. She would always be fond of him but she made no secret of her delight in this dark, handsome newcomer who had so much boldness and vitality. She had always been a good judge of men. She knew he was no idle courtier but a man of distinction whose ability and energy she meant to use to the advantage of her country.

If Walter had succeeded in catching the queen's interest, he had also to keep it. During that first year he was sometimes balanced on a knife-edge of insecurity. Her first gift gave him an income, but it was not nearly enough. She granted him estates in Ireland, and he plunged into a long-thought-out plan for the resettlement of tenants from his own West Country. Since the queen, however, would not let him leave her side, he was forced to work through his cousins in Devon. It would be a long time before his lands would show any profit.

Envy, spite, hostility met him at every step, but he ignored it. His very brilliance, the quality of difference that singled him out from other men, the fact that he rarely flattered or gathered a little band of supporters around him, made him distrusted. He was too proud, too sure of himself, too careless of what other people thought of him. For those he liked and respected he had always had a magnetic charm, but as for the rest . . . "If any man accuseth me to my face, I will answer him with my mouth, but my tail is good enough to return an answer to such as traduceth me behind my back."

"Upstart" and "adventurer" were the names they flung at him because he was not one of the old nobility. Aware of his own ancient line, he showed his resentment too openly for safety.

Already he was besieged by petitioners begging him for a word to the queen on their behalf. Even the great Lord Burghley asked him to intercede for his tiresome son-in-law the Earl of Oxford, who had offended Elizabeth. Walter had a quick sympathy for anyone he thought worthy or for the poor and the humble, who had nobody to speak for them, and he sometimes helped them to his own disadvantage. But he gave a very short answer to the hypocritical, the fools and liars, and it was they who were all too ready to take their revenge by slandering him.

Practically every penny he could spare was going into the

building of his first ship. He had long realized that the road to wealth and power was through trade, and for that he must establish a small fleet.

Sir John Hawkins, a wealthy merchant seaman of Plymouth, who had been placed in charge of the navy, had revolutionized the design of ships. In earlier times warships had been built like floating castles, their chief purpose to carry troops of soldiers. In battle the soldiers' aim was to grapple the ships against the enemy vessels, board them, and fight it out with sword and cutlass on the decks. But the great galleons were slow, unwieldy, and difficult to maneuver if the wind was against them. Hawkins, and his nephew Drake, had discovered the advantage of using smaller vessels.

Walter had developed these ideas further. Ships should be compactly built, low in the water, and well-armed, so that they could deliver a broadside into the enemy, then veer and tack in the wind till they could return and fire again from the other side. He also thought it necessary in these times for merchant ships to be as ready for battle as a warship.

Walter consulted Dr. John Dee, who, besides being an astrologer and a very learned man whom the queen herself consulted on occasion, was also an expert geographer with a great knowledge of navigation. In his study at Mortlake on the river Thames, they studied plans of construction that began to take shape in the yards of Peter Pett, the royal shipwright at Deptford.

Walter had recruited a young scientist from Oxford to help him with his mathematical studies and navigational problems. Thomas Hariot was twenty-one, a gentle, quiet young man. It did not take Walter long to recognize the original genius beneath the shy manner. Though funds were still very scarce, he generously invited Hariot to share his household, and a warm friendship sprang up between them.

Crowded as his life had become, in constant attendance on the queen, pursuing every modern fashion, every new trend in thought, he had still not forgotten the dream he shared with Humphrey of settling an English colony in the land across the Atlantic. At the very first opportunity he used his new-found favor to draw the queen's attention to his half brother's ambitious plans.

Elizabeth did not share their passionate interest. She expected her seamen to bring her gold, an immediate profit. To her way of thinking, Humphrey and Walter would be wasting ships, money, and probably lives for a barren stretch of land that would cost her a fortune to maintain. But Walter persisted and early in 1583 she yielded to his pleading and granted Humphrey the charter he had wanted for so long. But on one point she remained firm. Sea voyages were too dangerous. She would not permit Walter to risk his life by going with his brother as his vice-admiral.

He was bitterly disappointed. It would have been a fulfillment of the dream he had cherished since boyhood. But he was learning that he could not have the queen's favor and at the same time keep his independence. It was bittersweet to know her concern for him and at the same time to be denied what he wanted so passionately.

On March 17, 1583, he wrote to Humphrey from Richmond Palace: "Brother, I have sent you a token from Her Majesty, an anchor guided by a lady as you can see, and farther, Her Majesty willed me to send you word that she wished you as great good hap and safety to your ship, as if she herself was there in person, desiring you to have care of yourself, as of that which she tendereth; and therefore, for her sake, you must provide for it accordingly."

His new ship, the *Bark Ralegh*, which he had longed to command himself, was to sail with Humphrey.

In August of that year Walter was with the queen at the Palace of Oatlands when the first report came from Newfoundland. Humphrey had triumphantly set up the royal arms engraved on lead on a pillar of wood proclaiming England's first dominion overseas. But three months later, when the court was back at Whitehall, Captain Edward Hayes arrived from Cornwall with tragic news.

The expedition had sailed south from Newfoundland, exploring the coast of America, but then disaster had overtaken them. Storms arose, the water seemed to boil, running in all directions as if a thousand fiendish winds were blowing from all points of the compass. Fogs shut them in; their supply ship hit an uncharted reef and was lost with a hundred lives. There were arguments and disagreements among the captains, and Humphrey carried his admiral's flag to the *Squirrel*.

"Why the *Squirrel*?" asked Walter. "It was the smallest of all his ships."

Captain Hayes hesitated. "Some of his officers had jeered at him, hinting that he feared the sea's strength. You know Sir Humphrey's proud temper. To prove his courage he transferred to the frigate, which not one of them would have dared to do."

"What happened then?" asked the queen.

"We ran into the worst tempests I have known in those waters, Your Majesty. We besought Sir Humphrey to leave the overcrowded *Squirrel* and come on board our own ship, but he resolutely refused. 'I will not forsake my little company,' he

National Portrait Gallery

Sir Humphrey Gilbert as depicted in an early seventeenth-century engraving

said, 'with whom I have passed through so many perils.' The last sight we had of him, he was seated on the deck reading a book as calmly as if we had been sailing down the Thames. 'We are as near heaven at sea as on land,' he called out to us cheerfully. That same night the frigate was ahead of us when suddenly her lights went out. In a moment, it seemed, she was gone. Despite the racking of the winds, we searched the sea for survivors, but at midnight in those surging waters what could we have done?"

Walter sorrowed deeply for his brother's death. It did not seem possible that the gallant spirit whose daring motto had been *Quid Non?* ("Why not?") could be lost forever in the wild seas of the Atlantic. He was filled with a grim determination to carry out his brother's dream himself. He had a fierce contempt for the jeering fools who could send a man to his death with mockery. Humphrey should have laughed at them, but he understood his sensitive pride too well. It was part of himself.

5 : *"To seek new worlds for gold, for praise, for glory"*

—Walter Ralegh

Five months after Humphrey's death, Elizabeth granted Walter a six-year license to "discover, search, find out and view such remote, heathen and barbarous lands, countries and territories not actually possessed of any Christian prince, nor inhabited by Christian people."

A few weeks later he dispatched the *Bark Ralegh*, safely returned from Humphrey's expedition, and her new sister ship, the *Dorothy*, to explore the coast of America north of the Spanish outposts in Florida. After studying all available charts and reading everything that had been written by others on the subject, he had decided that this would be the best place to establish his future colony.

While he waited for them to return, he had plenty to occupy him. He tried hard to buy back Hayes, the beloved home of his childhood. He wrote to the present owner offering "most willingly to give you whatsoever in your conscience you shall deem it worth." But the wealthy Mr. Duke saw no reason why he should please the queen's upstart favorite and obstinately refused to sell. Walter's disappointment was keen, but during the summer Elizabeth granted him a home in London.

Durham House was an old, rambling building, part Norman castle, sprawling along the Strand, with gardens and orchards stretching down to the river. He explored it with delight. From the windows in the bare dusty room at the top of the turret he could see up the Thames to Whitehall and downriver to London Bridge. The air blew in fresh and sweet, and he decided that this should be his study, where he would keep his books, his charts, his great globe of the world turning on its stand, all the things he valued most.

It became the room he loved best, where he talked with his intimate friends, where he wrote his poetry, where he studied—sometimes rising at five in the morning because his days were so full there was little time left for reading—and where he relaxed in the very few minutes that he allowed himself such indulgence. He had horses in his stables and a staff of servants, and he could entertain in the way he preferred, small intimate supper parties where the conversation ranged over widely different subjects.

Thomas Hariot had his own room there and set up a twelve-foot perspective glass on the roof so that he could observe the polestar and improve navigation rules for Walter's sea captains. Hariot had already revised the old charts. He pointed out that in the past they had never taken into consideration the curve of the earth's surface, so that a ship could be miles away from where her captain believed her to be. Now, following Hariot's corrections, their calculations could be far more exact.

George Carew and Arthur Gorges were constantly in and out when they were in London. Richard Hakluyt, who was still seeking material for his great book, which would one day become *The Principal Navigations of the English People*, had gone as chaplain to the embassy in Paris, and Walter recklessly spent £60 on the manuscript of the Portuguese Vasco da Gama's voyage to the Red Sea in 1541 and sent it off in triumph to his friend in France.

Dr. Dee came to dine, bringing with him some of the amusing mechanical toys he had bought in Germany, a giant beetle that crawled all over the table, an owl and a raven that hooted and cawed just like real birds. The servants were scared out of their wits. "It's witchcraft," they muttered to one another, because Dr. Dee had the reputation of a sorcerer as well as of an authority on Euclid and astronomy. He had a glass made of obsidian, a black volcanic stone, in which he was said to be able to see the future. "It's magic," people mumbled, shuddering, afraid to speak too loudly in case it should bring them bad luck. Superstitious nonsense of this kind did not trouble Walter. He had already charmed the queen into remedying her neglect of the old man and easing his poverty.

About this time Walter made a new friend. Lawrence Keymis was a scholar of Balliol College, Oxford, but he was also passionately interested in exploration. He was enchanted to join the brilliant intellectual circle Walter had gathered around him, which discussed science and religion, poetry and philosophy, looking forward to new ideas and a new future when England's overseas empire should rival Spain's.

The surest way to win Walter's interest was originality of mind. In his great hall you might meet a needy poet, a West Country sea captain, some fascinating if doubtful foreigner, or a scholar with a new and daring theory to expound. In time

Durham House began to acquire a reputation for strange company, for dangerously modern thought and a disturbing lack of ordinary convention.

Walter's two ships came sailing home in September, and he went down to Plymouth to meet them and hear their officers' reports. Captain Arthur Barlow was filled with enthusiasm. They had landed on a sandy reef off the coast of what is now North Carolina.

"As we approached the land," he said, "we smelled so sweet and so strong a smell, it was as if we had been in the midst of some delicate garden. Grapes grow to the water's edge, covering every shrub and climbing to the treetops, while the woods have the very highest and reddest cedars in the world."

Exploring farther, they had found the land fertile and the climate good. They had traded with the Indians and found them "most gentle, loving, and faithful, void of all guile and treason, and such as live after the golden age."

They had brought two of the natives back with them on the ship. They were called Manteo and Wanchese. Walter took them with him to London and presented them to the queen. A young German, Leopold von Wedel, who was visiting the court that autumn, stared at them with wonder.

"In face and figure they were like white Moors," he wrote in his diary. "Normally they wear no shirt, just a wild animal skin across the shoulders and a strip of fur around their waist, but now they were dressed in brown taffeta. No one could understand what they said and altogether they looked very childish and uncouth."

Encouraged by the optimistic reports he had received, Walter wanted to begin at once to plan his first colonizing voyage, which would carry emigrants to make their home in the uninhabited stretches of this wonderful new world. But first there

Trustees of the British Museum

The arrival of the English in Virginia. Engraving by Theodore de Bry after a drawing by John White, official artist of the expedition

were the twelve days of Christmas to be celebrated at the Palace of Greenwich.

Von Wedel, still in England, described the queen in his diary. She wore black velvet sumptuously embroidered in silver and pearls, and diamonds in her hair; and a long veil like a tissue of gossamer fell to her feet. The dancing began with the pavane, a slow stately measure that the queen performed with an exquisite grace. Then the young courtiers laid aside their cloaks and swords and in doublet and hose invited the maids of honor to dance the gay, lively galliard, followed by the volta, where the young men tossed their partners into the air so their satin skirts flew up and revealed slender ankles in silken stockings of crimson, green, white, and tawny. The prim young German was very shocked.

"During the dancing," he wrote with strong disapproval, "the queen summoned young and old to come and talk with her. They all knelt to her and she chatted in a very friendly way, making jokes. She said to a captain named Ralegh, pointing with her finger at his face, that there was a smut on it, and was going to wipe it off with her handkerchief but before she could, he wiped it off himself. She was said to love this gentleman now beyond all others; and this may be true, because two years ago he could scarcely keep one servant and now with her bounty, he can keep five hundred."

It was not quite true, but certainly Walter had come a very long way toward fulfilling his ambitions.

Increasing prosperity had brought a degree of luxury into the court that horrified the Puritan preachers. The ladies were actually using perfume, they thundered in outrage from their pulpits, "the smell whereof may be perceived not only all over the place, but a stone's throw off." Their ruffs too, trimmed with gold or silver and edged with the finest lace, "sparkled and sparked here and there with the sun, the moon, and the stars."

Most magnificent of them all at court was the "queen's dear minion," as they called Walter spitefully. On the Feast of the Three Kings, the last day of the Christmas revels, when the queen knighted him, he outshone everyone with the splendor of his black velvet cloak embroidered with silver and sewn with pearls. His pale satin doublet was fastened with emeralds, Elizabeth's favorite gem, and he wore a single pearl earring, a new fashion that immediately became all the rage among the young men.

The knighthood meant a great deal to him. The queen was careful of her honors. She bestowed them only on those she considered worthy. As she touched his shoulder with the ceremonial sword, she thought what a man of contrasts he was. At that moment he looked a very peacock of fashion from the lustrous dark hair to the jewels on his shoes, but already one of his ships had captured a prize that had brought her a fine cargo of gold and pearls. She had read the report he had brought her; she had listened with interest to him talking about the empire he meant to give her across the seas; she had graciously consented that he might call his new colony Virginia after herself, the Virgin Queen, but she had little patience with the plans he was pursuing so eagerly. Her seamen had been bringing her madcap schemes for years, and her keen practical mind was inclined to judge them too ambitious, too vague, too impossible to realize. Let Walter squander his own money if he wished. In the meantime she had other plans for him.

Walter had a new seal made inscribed "Walter Ralegh Knight, Lord and Governor of Virginia," and within it his arms surmounted by a roebuck and the motto *Amore et Virtute* ("With Love and Courage"). His love for the queen and hers for him flowed into a new poem:

> Silence in love bewrays more woe
> > Than words, though ne'er so witty;
> A beggar that is dumb, you know,
> > Deserveth double pity.
> Then misconceive not, dearest heart,
> > My true, though secret passion.
> He smarteth most that hides his smart
> > And sues for no compassion.

During 1585 Elizabeth appointed him Lord Lieutenant of Cornwall, Vice-Admiral of Devon and Cornwall, and Lord Warden of the Stannaries, making him at one stroke of the pen the most powerful man in the West of England. Cornwall and Devon were the likeliest area for Spanish raids and invasions, an ever-present fear. Walter was in charge of naval and military defenses, an immensely responsible position.

As Warden of the Stannaries, he controlled the tin industry, which was of great value and importance. Cornish tin had been exported since before the Romans came to England. Even the Turks bought it, for smelting with copper and making their bronze guns.

The tin miners earned £3 a year laboring in hot, damp, dangerous underground workings by the light of a single candle stuck in their caps. They were the poorest, toughest, and most independent body of men in England, owing allegiance only to their own leaders and their own parliament. Their courts were held in the heart of Dartmoor on Crocken Tor, and here Walter sat with them in an ancient circle of great stones like a tribal chieftain and heard their grievances in a desolation so high and lonely that often they were hidden by the thick mists that swirled around them. He fought hard for their rights and privileges and did his best to get their miserable wages doubled.

As so often happens with those in authority, he was criticized and slandered, but later at one of the most wretched moments of his life, when he was imprisoned in the Tower of London, Richard Carew dedicated his *Survey of Cornwall* to him, expressing gratitude for his good work throughout the years: "Your ears and mouth have ever been open to hear and deliver our grievances, and your feet and hands ready to go and work their redress, and that, not only always as a magistrate, or yourself, but also very often as a suitor and solicitor of others of the highest place."

Whatever hatred and jealousy surrounded him up in London, in the West Country he was loved and respected. To the people of Devon and Cornwall, he was not the magnificent courtier with his diamond hatband and his rich satins, but one of their own, a man who spoke to them in the West Country accent they knew. What he said was clear and sensible, not high-flown oratory a plain man could not understand. He had grown up with them, he was aware of their problems and he fought for them in Parliament.

He had to appoint deputies, one of whom was Humphrey's elder brother, Sir John Gilbert. His own brother, Carew, became deputy Warden of the Stannaries, but Walter did not govern from a distance. He took his duties seriously and carried them out conscientiously. All through the years he held office, he was constantly riding the three hundred miles between the court and Devon and Cornwall.

He had very soon begun to realize that the colonizing venture on which he had set his heart would require more money than any private person could hope to possess. But when a start had been made he felt confident that he would be able to persuade the queen to approve his project and make the long-term investment herself. In the meantime he added the *Roebuck*, the *Black Dog*, and the *Mary Spark* to his small fleet of ships and sent them out to trade and to capture the rich Spanish merchantmen with their valuable cargoes. He made sure to keep everything under his own control. He briefed the captains, planned the voyages, issued the orders, and as far as was possible made himself personally known to the crews.

During the early months of 1585 while he gathered men, ships, and money, it had been in his mind to command the first American colonizing expedition himself, but however much he pleaded, that was the one thing the queen would not permit. She had raised him to high position and in return he must stay always at her side. She promised to lend him one of her own ships provided that he did not sail in her, and so in the end they set out from Plymouth on April 9 without him. His cousin, Sir Richard Grenville, took his place in the *Tyger* and was accompanied by *Roebuck, Lion, Elizabeth,* and *Dorothy*, carrying 107 settlers—farmers, carpenters, plowmen, craftsmen of all kinds, and gentlemen volunteers eager for adventure under a governor, Ralph Lane. Thomas Hariot was with them as scientific expert to collect and examine vegetable and mineral products and to study the Indians, the agriculture, and trade prospects. With them also went John White, an artist, who would draw up the maps and record in charming watercolors the plants, animals, and native life.

It would be many months before he could hope to hear from them, so Walter went back to London, to the stifling atmos-

An American Indian, dressed for hunting or feasting, as drawn by John White

phere of the court and to the queen who still enchanted him, though sometimes he rebelled against the chains with which she bound him to her.

Leicester had gone to the Netherlands as lieutenant general of the army. The great Protestant leader William of Orange had been assassinated the previous year, and the people of Holland implored Elizabeth's help against the oppression of the Spaniards and the tortures of the Inquisition.

All that year Walter was first favorite, so close to Elizabeth that one evening when Richard Tarleton, the celebrated little clown, was entertaining the court with some of his saucy jests, he pointed to the tall dark figure standing beside the queen's chair and said with a sneer, "See, the knave commands the queen."

Elizabeth frowned and rebuked him for his insolence, but there were plenty who rejoiced at it. Not that Walter cared a jot for any of them. He walked through the court confident of the queen's affection and with nothing but contempt for the backbiters and slanderers who fawned on him to his face and tore him to shreds behind his back.

Tragedy touched the royal circle in the summer of 1586 when Sir Philip Sidney, who had gone with his uncle to the Netherlands, was wounded at the battle of Zutphen. The story of his gallantry was often repeated at court. Exhausted by loss of blood and parched with thirst, he was brought a bottle of water. As he raised it to his lips, he saw the agonized longing in the eyes of a foot soldier being carried past him, and without drinking he handed it to the dying man saying, "Thy necessity is yet greater than mine."

All England mourned the death of the chivalrous young man and Walter's elegy caught the public note of grief:

> A kingly mind
> That God thee gave is now too dear
> For this base world. . . .
> Let Angels speak and Heaven thy praises tell.

That same year Walter suffered a cruel disappointment. His first colonial enterprise had been a dismal failure. In July the whole body of colonists packed up and returned to England.

"What went wrong?" he asked Thomas Hariot, pacing impatiently up and down his study at the first opportunity they had to be alone. "I exerted every effort to send off supply ships in April with everything the colony could possibly need for another year."

"They arrived too late," said Hariot sadly. "When Francis Drake on his way back from Florida called into Chesapeake Bay and offered to give passage to those who wished to return, most of them were all too eager to abandon their holdings and run home."

"Is the country so uninhabitable?"

"The land is fair and good, the climate gentle, better than in England, and we did not suffer from Indian attack at first. But there were some among the settlers who could not live in peace. The Indians would have been ready enough to trade, but unfortunately one of them stole a silver cup. The colonists retaliated savagely, and after one of their villages had been raided and their women and children killed, the Indians naturally took revenge."

"I warned them of that," said Walter bitterly. "Again and again I stressed that they should not ill-treat the Indians or attack them without extreme provocation. Friendship with the natives is the only way to peaceful settlement."

Trustees of the British Museum

The Indian village of Secoton, as drawn by John White

If only he had been able to go with them himself, he thought, he was sure he would have been able to inspire them to greater efforts. He knew his own power over men and how he could have persuaded them not to give up but go on and achieve their dream. He had learned himself that nothing in this life comes easily.

"I thought I was giving an opportunity to men who longed for freedom, a new land where they could work out their own lives," he went on.

"They are not ready for it, Walter," answered Hariot. "When some of the settlers discovered that gold and silver were not to be found immediately, they had no care for anything else. There were others who grew discontented because they did not find fine houses like those at home with soft feather beds and the food to which they were accustomed. They thought it beneath them to till the ground or sow the crops that would have secured their future."

All they thought of was gold. If only he could make them understand how little that mattered compared with the triumph of founding a new land. What Walter wanted was a firm foothold for his countrymen on the northern continent of America that would balance the power of the Spaniards in the south.

Despite his failure, he refused to give up. He immediately set to work planning a second expedition, this time under a strong governor. He chose John White, the artist, who had been fascinated by the New World and had shown himself both capable and intelligent. He would be supported by a council of twelve. They would found a community with the rights of self-government under their leaders, and he himself would give them such explicit instructions that surely this time nothing could go wrong.

All that winter he worked on his plans, gathering a company of 150 settlers who would sail with their wives and families. But in the meantime trouble mounted throughout the kingdom.

For years now Elizabeth had gone in danger of assassination. In 1570 the Pope had issued a papal bull in Rome proclaiming her a heretic and calling upon every loyal Catholic to bring about her destruction so that England might be brought back to the true faith. It had intensified religious strife. Catholic priests who came secretly to England to say mass and carry the sacraments to the faithful were hunted down and barbarously executed, not so much for their religious beliefs as for possible treason against the state.

Like Walter, Elizabeth had tolerant views on religion. "I desire to open a window on no man's conscience," she said more than once. "There is only one God and only one religion and the rest is a dispute about trifles," was her impatient reply to those who argued about small points of doctrine. Provided that her subjects remained loyal to England, she would have let men of any belief live in peace, but her council, her Parliament, and her people would not allow her to be merciful. Memories of the massacre on Saint Bartholomew's Day still haunted them; they lived in fear that their beloved queen would be murdered by some crazy fanatic. Mary Queen of Scots might be a prisoner, but she was a Catholic and through her grandmother, Margaret, sister to Henry VIII, she was the rightful heir to the throne if Elizabeth should die. For that very reason she was the center of every Catholic plot.

During the summer of that year the scheming and discontent, like a long-festering boil, came to a head and burst. But Sir Francis Walsingham, through his intricate network of spies, had watched every move, read every hidden message, unraveled every knot.

"To seek new worlds for gold, for praise, for glory" : 65

All during these anxious weeks while he waited until he had gathered all into his net, Elizabeth came very near to death. It was a nerve-racking time. She refused to change her habit of going about her palaces and gardens unguarded, and any one of the six chief conspirators had access to her court. At last Walsingham pounced. Anthony Babington, a young Catholic with a romantic devotion to the Scottish queen, was arrested with his confederates. They were tried and condemned to death. But the real importance was the final bringing home of her guilt to Mary of Scotland.

In their anxiety all her councilors, Walter among them, besought Elizabeth to rid herself of the woman who had caused so much unrest in the kingdom for so many years, but it was a long time before she would consent to Mary's trial. In the end, though she realized the necessity, she signed the death warrant only under pressure from Burghley and the Privy Council.

On a cold frosty morning in February 1587, when Elizabeth returned to Greenwich from her usual morning ride, she heard the bells ringing out from London Town. Bonfires were blazing in the streets. A messenger brought the news. The Queen of Scots had been executed at Fotheringhay Castle and the people were shouting their joy.

Elizabeth felt only grief and regret. "I envied her the son she bore and now I have rendered him motherless," she said. A monarch was anointed by God. It was an ideal of royalty that had been sacred to her all her life, but in addition to that belief was something more horrible. To cut off the head of a queen awoke the memory of her own mother, Anne Boleyn, who had died under the headsman's sword, a memory that had haunted her childhood. The execution reminded her also of her father's fifth wife, the gay and pretty Catherine Howard, who had been kind to the lonely, motherless little Elizabeth until the fearful day when she too went to her death on the block.

"I never saw her fetch a sigh but when the Queen of Scots was beheaded," wrote one of Elizabeth's young courtiers at this time.

But to the people of England it was as if a black cloud had rolled away, and they sighed with relief. Everywhere a new song was being sung to a strange and frightening air by the queen's musician William Byrd:

> The noble famous queen
> Who lost her head of late
> Doth show that kings as well as clowns
> Are bound to Fortune's fate,
> And that no earthly prince
> Can so secure his crown
> But Fortune with her whirling wheel
> Hath power to pull them down.

6 : *"That Morris Dance upon the Waters"*

—Sir Henry Wotton

Walter had been appointed Captain of the Guard, a post of the highest distinction and trust, since it gave him the privilege of being always in the queen's presence. The uniform was dull and uninteresting, but he ordered a suit of armor plated with finely engraved silver from Joseph Halder, master smith at the Greenwich Foundry. It cost a small fortune. The queen scolded him for his wild extravagance when he appeared in it for the first time, but in the spring of 1587 Walter was at a high peak of favor and it seemed that nothing could go wrong.

His new expedition had left Plymouth early in May. Colonization was in the air. Everyone was talking about it, some enviously, a great many scornfully. How could any sensible person believe that such a crazy scheme would ever succeed?

At the Rose Theatre over the river in Southwark, Edward

Alleyn, the actor, was thundering out the mighty lines of *Tamburlaine*, about the great conqueror whose chariot was drawn by six captive kings. Christopher Marlowe's play had been a tremendous success. He had lately become acquainted with Thomas Hariot and hovered hopefully on the edge of the Ralegh circle.

All that spring Hariot himself had been busy writing a report on Virginia, this fabulous new land where flax and hemp grew in abundance, where it would be possible to develop a trade with pitch, tar, turpentine, and red cedarwood, where copper and iron could be mined. In Paris, Hakluyt was paying enthusiastic tribute to Walter's far-reaching plans for this country of boundless opportunity.

Michael Drayton, the poet, burst into praise of the Virginian explorers:

> You brave heroic minds,
> Worthy your country's name,
>   That honour still pursue.
>   Go and subdue,
> Whilst loit'ring hinds
> Lurk here at home with shame
> And cheerfully at sea
> Success you still entice
>   To get the pearl and gold
>   And ours to hold,
> Virginia,
> Earth's only paradise.

In June, Walter had the pleasure of seeing his new ship, the *Ark Ralegh*, launched at Deptford. She was larger than any he had ordered so far and built entirely according to his own design. The queen saw the ship lying in the Thames as she went down

Ark Royal, formerly *Ark Ralegh*. Anonymous woodcut of the late sixteenth century

to Greenwich in her barge and sent the Lord High Admiral to look her over. The great man grunted and grumbled as he followed Walter from forecastle to stern. He wasn't sure he trusted all these new ideas, but all the same he advised the queen to buy the *Ark* and privately made up his mind to take her for his own flagship. Ruefully, Walter saw her name changed to *Ark Royal* and wondered if he would ever receive from Elizabeth the £5,000 the *Ark* had cost him.

To one young man newly come to court that summer, it seemed that the name Walter Ralegh was on everyone's lips.

Robert Devereux, Earl of Essex, was Leicester's stepson. He was just twenty, tall, handsome in a boyish way, with red-gold hair and blue eyes. His great-grandmother had been Anne Boleyn's sister, which made him distant cousin to the queen. He was the poorest earl in England, but through his father he was descended from noble families of medieval times and was intensely proud of his ancient lineage.

Elizabeth was delighted with his good looks, his youthful charm, and his high spirits. She welcomed him at once into her intimate circle. But the young man had been petted and spoiled by his adoring mother and devoted sisters. He accepted favors as no more than his right, was gay or moody as it suited him, sulked if he did not get his own way, and very quickly resented anyone else whom the queen smiled upon. A young courtier to whom she had given a golden chessman turned up at court one day with the token proudly bound to his arm with a blue ribbon.

"Now I perceive every fool must wear a favor," remarked Essex insolently. In a moment they were quarreling, a duel followed, and Essex was slightly wounded.

But it was Walter who from the very first aroused his furious jealousy.

One evening Essex stood watching the merry group around the queen. Walter was demonstrating his latest craze for smoking the Indian weed called tobacco, which Hariot had brought back from Virginia. He filled his long, silver-bound pipe and puffed out the smoke while the maids of honor giggled at such an extraordinary spectacle. Then the queen had to try it herself, though Lord Burghley shook his head in grave doubt. She took an experimental puff, choked, and tried again successfully. Walter remarked dryly, "The first time I smoked a pipe, my servant was so sure I was burning in hellfire, he poured a mug of ale over my head."

All the ladies-in-waiting had to have their turn, and while the pipe went from one to the other, Walter said smiling, "What will Your Majesty bet me that I cannot weigh my own tobacco smoke?"

Elizabeth rapped his cheek for his impertinence, but she loved a wager and felt sure he could not win. She nodded her agreement. He called for a pair of scales, carefully weighed a pipeful of tobacco, smoked it, weighed the ash and triumphantly announced the difference.

The queen, crowing with laughter, handed over the money, exclaiming wryly that, though she had known several alchemists turn gold into smoke with their expensive experiments, he was the first to turn smoke into gold.

Essex leaned against the wall with folded arms, smoldering inside that this dark, magnificent man should be on such familiar terms with the queen, that he should stroll about the court, so elegant and self-assured, that he wrote poetry so full of passion and vigor that it made his own verses sound like mere doggerel.

That summer it was intensely hot, but Elizabeth went on a progress as usual, moving tirelessly from castle to country house, and her courtiers went with her. One evening Essex let his smoldering resentment flare into open hostility. He came bursting into the room where Elizabeth had retired to rest, falling on his knees and crying out that she had wronged him.

Walter, on guard at the door, could not hear everything that was said, only that the earl was attacking him and that the queen had flown to his defense.

Then Essex deliberately raised his voice. "What pleasure can there be in the service of a mistress who goes in awe of such a man as Walter Ralegh?"

He should have known by this time that to slander anyone she was fond of was a sure way to the queen's displeasure.

"Let be," she answered sharply. "I will hear no more."

Essex lost his head completely. "What joy can I have in being near you," he went on recklessly, "when my love is cast away and so vile a wretch as Ralegh is so highly esteemed by you."

But this time he had gone too far. The queen angrily turned her back on him and Essex came storming out of the room, thrusting rudely past Walter. He called for his horses and rode furiously away, swearing that he would take ship for Holland, to fight and die in the Dutch wars.

"By God's death!" exclaimed Elizabeth impatiently. "It were time someone should take him down and teach him better manners." And she sent one of her gentlemen galloping after him. He was brought back and severely reprimanded like a naughty child. If possible, his hatred of his rival grew even more fierce.

Walter laughed over the incident with his new friend, Robert Cecil. Cecil, Lord Burghley's younger son, had only recently come to court. He was twenty-four, small, slight, frail, almost a hunchback. His childhood had been made miserable by envy of his more fortunate companions. All his cleverness, all his success at the university could never quite make up for the fact that he could not ride or swim or play tennis; he could not dance or hope to please a pretty girl.

He smiled at Walter's tale but said nothing. Robert Cecil never wasted words and he had his own private reasons for disliking Essex. The young earl's father had died when he was nine years old and he had been brought up as Burghley's ward. How often in their country home in Hertfordshire he had flaunted his youth and beauty, his skill at riding and swordplay, before the sensitive crippled boy. It is not easy to forget such hurts. It had made Robert Cecil afraid of friendship, but with Walter it was different.

Cecil's father had once cautioned him in a letter, "It is mere folly for a man to enthrall himself to his friend as though, occasion being offered, he should not dare to become his enemy." But he found it hard to remember when Walter threw an arm around his shoulders, treating him as an equal, making him feel one with all the brilliant men who circled around the queen. It helped to take away the sting of her nickname for him. Her "Pygmy," she called him. Though she had not meant it unkindly, how could a man feel anything but pain.

Essex came back to court and to the queen's favor. She made him Master of the Horse and hung the blue ribbon of the Garter around his neck. A great many who disliked Walter rejoiced to see this. "Nobody near her but my lord of Essex," one of them wrote home. "And at night my lord is at cards or one game or another with her till the birds sing in the morning."

Essex's touchy temper was causing quarrels to flare up everywhere. Walter made the mistake of losing patience with him and was challenged to a duel, which the council stepped in to prevent before it got to the ears of the queen.

Essex had gathered a little band of flatterers around him only too happy to support the rising star. Walter had always stood alone. He was suddenly very aware of the attack upon his position. The court was like a jungle, he thought. You needed to have eyes and ears all around you. For the first time since the queen had favored him, he felt his confidence shaken. But then the whole situation was forgotten in the threat of war. He lost his private anxieties in the public duties thrust upon him.

For years Elizabeth had preserved her country's peace. Openly she was on the best of terms with Philip of Spain, writing to him as her dear friend and signing herself his loving sister. The expeditions of Drake and Hawkins or Walter's little fleet that hunted down the Spanish merchantmen were all private ventures, though the gold and jewels poured into her treasure chests.

But these conditions could not last. Drake's last expedition had amounted to open war. With a small squadron he had sailed into Cadiz harbor, burned thousands of tons of ships and stores, seized Cape St. Vincent to prevent the Spanish fleet gathering there, and captured a treasure ship worth £114,000. This was clear defiance of all neutrality, and in his lonely palace in the rocky hills of Guadarrama, King Philip was slowly making plans to destroy the heretic queen and her small island nation.

Rumors of the great Armada he was collecting had been filtering into England for months now, gathered from Walsingham's spies, from Walter's sea captains, from Hawkins' merchantmen. Tales of the Inquisition and the tortures endured by soldiers and seamen who had been shipwrecked and made prisoner grew with each telling. Hatred of the Catholics rose higher and higher until it seemed that everyone not of the reformed faith must be Spanish at heart and a traitor to England.

"No war, gentlemen," Elizabeth had said to her council again and again, and for thirty years she had avoided it by lies, evasions, intrigue, and the skillful handling of the balance of power, but now there was no escape. In the spring of 1588 Walter sat on a council of war to discuss the best method of meeting the threatened invasion.

He pleaded to be allowed to command his own heavily armed *Roebuck* and join the fleet under Admiral Howard and Drake, but his request was refused. His influence in the West Country was far too valuable.

Only a few days before the council of war met, John White had returned from Virginia. He had been sent back by the colonists to beg for stores and provisions to help them live through the coming year. There had been trouble with the Indians, he told Walter, though he himself had tried hard to carry out Walter's farsighted aims at friendship with the native tribes and peace had been patched up before he left. "My daughter has borne a child," he added proudly. "The first English citizen to be born in the New World, and we have christened her Virginia."

But it was a bad time to find the necessary supplies. All available shipping was being held in England against Spanish invasion. With the utmost difficulty Walter fitted out two small ships with the stores the colony needed, but the crews had little heart for the long, dangerous voyage. Attacked by pirates, they gave up and fled back to Plymouth. For the moment it was impossible for Walter to do more. He had no time to spare for anything but preparations for defense. The musters of men had to be called up, Devon and Cornwall must be armed and ready, the giant beacons built on the hills to give warning when the Armada was sighted. His tin miners volunteered to a man, but in the towns he met with the usual blank refusal to recognize danger until it is on the doorstep, and he fought it with every ounce of energy he had.

He toured the coastal defenses, inspecting every fortification personally and was in Portland at the end of July when the Armada was glimpsed. Great bonfires blazed from the Lizard to Dover as 130 great galleons, with their attendant pinnaces and flyboats, moved slowly up the English Channel.

All the gilded youth of England raced to the coast to see the spectacle, even Robert Cecil, who could never hope to take an active part. Walter, as soon as danger to the West was gone, rode to London and begged to be allowed to join the fleet. At last he was sent with Richard Grenville to guard the western shores with a small squadron.

The Armada was met by the English fleet led by Admiral Howard in the *Ark Royal*, Drake in the *Revenge*, Hawkins in the *Victory*, and Frobisher in the *Triumph*. They fought their way up the Channel, the agile island ships with their expert gunnery attacking and retreating like small vicious dogs, doing crippling damage to the slower, more unwieldy galleons of the Spanish.

It was August before the Admiral could write to Walsingham, "Their force is wonderfully great and strong, and yet we pluck their feathers little by little."

The whole country was seething with excitement. Elizabeth went down to Tilbury to review her land army under Leicester's command. Her councilors had tried to prevent her, fearing treachery or assassination, but she would not listen to them. Wearing a silver corselet and riding on a white horse with Leicester on her right hand, Essex on her left, she spoke memorably.

"I do not desire to live to distrust my faithful and loving people. Let tyrants fear. . . . I am resolved in the midst and

The Spanish Armada, 1588 by an unknown artist roughly contemporary with the event. The painting shows the fighting in the English Channel; on the right is a stern view of the *Ark Royal*

National Maritime Museum, Greenwich

heat of the battle to live or die amongst you all. I know I have the body of a weak, feeble woman; but I have the heart and stomach of a king and of a king of England too."

She could be exasperating, demanding, difficult, thought Walter, but by God, she lit a flame in the heart of her people.

Though at first it seemed unbelievable, the great Armada was defeated. On one of the medals struck to commemorate the victory were inscribed the words, "God breathed and they were scattered." It was the strong gales that suddenly came up that finally scattered the crippled Spanish galleons and drove them up the North Sea. The broken remains of the Armada rounded the Shetland Isles and fled down the Irish coast, many of them foundering on the shores, where the inhabitants plundered their cargoes and murdered the crews. The Duke of Medina Sidonia led the pitiful remnant back to Spain.

"With all their great and terrible ostentation," wrote Walter, "they did not in all their sailing around England so much as sink or take one ship, bark, pinnace, or cockboat of ours, or ever burnt so much as one sheepcote of this land."

7 : "The Summer's Nightingale"

—Edmund Spenser

Walter returned to court in March of 1589. The queen thanked him for his services, hung a gold chain around his neck, and shut him out of her intimate circle. It was a shock and unbearably painful. His pride and his ambitions suffered a setback, but it was more than that. For seven years he had served her with love and devotion. He had been her willing captive, always at her beck and call; now he had to stand aside and watch another take the place that had been his.

He had known that the sudden death of Leicester, coming in the midst of the victory celebrations, would have been a shattering blow, but he never realized that, lonely and heartsick, Elizabeth would turn to Leicester's stepson, that it would be Essex with his youth and boyish charm who would take her heart

National Portrait Gallery

Robert Devereux, 2nd Earl of Essex

away from him. The rivalry between them broke into open conflict. For the first time Walter quarreled with the queen and received the lash of her tongue. He would not bend his pride and grovel at her feet as other men did. On the edge of disgrace, he went to see her, magnificent in black and silver, his head held high, and asked for permission to visit his lands in Ireland. Still angry with him, she let him go and then turned on Essex, attacking him for flaunting his triumph over his rival.

In Munster, Walter's tenant farmers were prospering, but his steward still had a long list of complaints for him to deal with. He had tried to persuade them to plant the potato, the new root from America that everyone but himself thought utterly unappetizing but that he was convinced would be a valuable foodstuff in time of famine. Now they grumbled lest the unfamiliar crop should fail. Even his gardeners complained because he insisted on them growing the flowers his captains brought him, lilacs from Persia and sweet-scented yellow wallflowers from the Azores. Why were men so tiresomely set in the old ways?

He dealt with the problems with his usual energy and set about finding himself somewhere to live. He was rebuilding Lismore Castle, but it was still too large and drafty for comfort. At the top of the steep, straggling high street of the port of Youghal, whose citizens had elected him mayor, he found a charming red-brick manor house. It reminded him of his childhood home at Hayes, and he settled himself there. His days were fully occupied with work on his estates and the new industries he was putting in hand, but the evenings seemed endless. At some moments he felt bitterly that he had devoted all his best years to a woman who had rejected him. Night after night he poured his feelings into grave, unhappy verses:

> She hath left me here all alone
> All alone as unknown
> Who sometime did me lead with herself
> And me loved as her own.

He would throw down his pen, feeling stifled in this remote country place, longing for the stimulation of the court and the elegant, fascinating woman who was the living heart of it.

But there were times when Ireland exerted her spell; the gentle green countryside was soothing, the warm rain-soft air relaxing. One day, on impulse, he rode along the banks of the Blackwater and knocked at the gate of Kilcolman Castle, home of Edmund Spenser.

Spenser was thirty-seven, a gentle, brown-haired man, who had been secretary to Lord Grey during the Irish wars and had been granted lands in Ireland for his services. He stared in astonishment at his distinguished visitor. He remembered well the aggressive Captain Ralegh whom his master had so much disliked. He had heard tales of the queen's favorite, of his arrogance, his ambitious grasping after power and wealth. It was difficult to believe them when Walter smiled at him, holding out his hand, telling him how much he had admired his long poem, *The Shepherd's Calendar,* inviting him to visit and bring his latest work with him.

The poet's heart leaped. Now that Lord Grey had left Ireland, he had no patron to put in an influential word for him, and Sir Walter was well known for the help and encouragement he gave to writers.

It became the habit for them to spend evenings together. The study in Walter's house in Youghal was paneled in dark bog oak, the finely carved mantelpiece reaching to the ceiling. Sunk deep in his chair, long legs stretched out, his pipe forgotten in his hand, Walter would listen to Spenser reading from *The Faerie Queene*. He thought it was a masterpiece. Afterward, at the poet's urging, he would bring out some of his own verses. They would spend so much time discussing questions of rhyme, alliteration, and meter that Spenser found it difficult to believe that his host was not a dedicated poet like himself.

At the end of the year, when Walter returned to London, he took Spenser with him. Elizabeth raised her eyebrows when the poet was presented to her. "Is this *Faerie Queene* so great a work?" she asked dryly, but she listened to Walter's urging.

The Faerie Queene was to be dedicated to her and published in January, and Spenser was to receive a pension of £50 a year.

Lord Burghley was shocked. "All that for a song, Your Majesty!" he grunted and looked disapprovingly at Walter.

Elizabeth was smiling with all her old affection. "When will you cease to be a beggar, Walter?" she asked.

"When Your gracious Majesty ceases to be a benefactor," was the cheerful reply.

> To thee that art the Summer's Nightingale,
> Thy Sovereign Goddess's most dear delight

wrote Spenser in a grateful sonnet to Walter, and Elizabeth seemed to agree, for that Christmas at Greenwich she was as eager for Walter's company as she had ever been.

The seesaw of fortune had swung Walter up again just as it was about to swing Essex down. He had dared to marry in secret Philip Sidney's pretty widow and she was expecting a baby. When in the New Year the queen found him out, her rage was appalling to watch. Unmarried herself, she had never been able to endure the men she favored turning from her to love other women. She was a powerful and brilliant ruler with one of the keenest minds in Europe, yet she wept with anger and mortification over a rebellious young man of twenty-three who was not worth her little finger. She banished him and his wife from her court and turned to Walter for comfort.

It was now, when everything seemed to be going Walter's way, that something happened that was to hurl him into disgrace and alter the whole course of his life. It was quite simple, the kind of thing that comes to every man sooner or later, just as it had come to Essex. He fell in love.

Bess Throckmorton was one of the queen's maids of honor. She was twenty-three, the daughter of Sir Nicholas Throckmorton, who had once been Elizabeth's ambassador in Paris. He had died when she was six and her mother had married again. Her dearly loved brother Arthur was already at court, and to be chosen as one of the ladies-in-waiting was a great honor for a young girl from a country home.

The queen could be generous to her maids. If they pleased her, she would find them good husbands, dance at their wedding, stand godmother to the first baby. Bess's father had not been a rich man. Her dowry was small and she had always known she must be sensible and look not for romance but for a kind husband who would give her a comfortable home. To fall in love with the queen's handsome favorite was a folly that she knew she should avoid but it was not easy to be sensible when this dark, fascinating man singled her out from all the others for his attentions.

As Captain of the Guard Walter was brought into close contact with the queen's ladies, but up till now had taken little notice of them. Frivolous girlish chatter bored him. He would dance with them, pay them charming compliments, and leave them for more interesting company. But now it was different.

National Gallery of Ireland

Lady Ralegh (Bess Throckmorton)

Bess was tall, golden-haired, and blue-eyed. She was not highly educated or clever or witty like the queen, but she had a warmth, a simplicity, a frank generous manner that drew him to her. She was not like the others; she did not giggle and tease to try and attract his attention. For this very reason he began to seek her out.

Of course her companions all warned her against him. "Have you forgotten how he insulted us?" Mary Howard reminded her. "He said, 'The queen's maids are like witches. They can do harm but very little good.'"

"He is in love with the queen," murmured another spitefully. "She will murder him if he so much as smiles at anyone else."

"He does not believe in God," whispered Elizabeth Brydges in a shocked voice. "You know what they call his circle at Durham House—the School of Atheism."

"Nonsense," Bess would reply indignantly, refusing to listen to their malicious gossip. "Some people will say anything."

But it was true that Walter entertained strange company in his study at the top of the tower. Christopher Marlowe, for instance, the shoemaker's son who had become such a successful playwright and whose new tragedy, *Doctor Faustus*, told the story of a man selling his soul to the devil for

> A world of profit and delight—
> Of power, of honour and omnipotence.

Rumor said that it was Sir Walter who had provided his inspiration. Marlowe had a bold, challenging intellect. He scoffed at the Bible. He laughed at religion. "Ignorance is the greatest sin," he used to say.

Then there was Henry Percy, Earl of Northumberland, who had the reputation of a wizard and was so passionately interested in chemistry that he had nearly blown himself up with one of his own experiments. "He'll be carried off by the Devil one of these days, likely as not," nervous people mumbled in the streets, and they took good care not to go too near his great house at Syon.

Twice that year Walter had pleaded passionately with the queen for men condemned to death for their religious beliefs. One, a Puritan, she pardoned; the other, a Catholic priest, not even Elizabeth could save from the hatred of the people.

It was not surprising that narrow-minded men distrusted Walter and scandalous rumors kept cropping up about him. Bess never could remember any of them when he was with her, though, fascinated by the charm that was so difficult to resist. Sometimes she tried to warn him, but he only laughed. He had utter scorn for the opinion of the crowd. "It is no more than the outcry of a herd of animals," he said contemptuously.

They were forced to keep their interest in one another secret from the queen. It was dangerous even to be seen talking together. But having to watch every step did not prevent them from falling deeper and deeper in love.

In the autumn John White, whom Walter had sent off with supply ships as soon after the Armada as possible, came back from Virginia with disastrous news. The colony he had left behind had vanished without trace. He didn't know whether they had been wiped out by the Spaniards or killed by the Indians or had wandered farther into the wilderness and died of starvation.

Later he was to write sadly, "The evils and unfortunate events had not chanced if the order set down by Sir Walter Ralegh had been observed."

Again and again Walter was to send out expeditions to hunt

for the lost colonists, but nothing was ever discovered. A tradition lingered for centuries that they had wandered off into the mountains to the west and intermarried with an Indian tribe, but this was never proved. Although Walter's first attempt at colonization had been a costly failure—he had spent time, energy, and £40,000, almost all his private fortune—he had not lost interest. The idea remained very close to his heart, but for the time being he could do no more. He turned his mind to other matters.

He had always been strongly opposed to Burghley's cautious policy toward Spain. Since its victory over the Armada, the island fleet had scoured the seas, burning and sinking Spanish ships where they could. Now the more adventurous spirits urged the queen to consent to a planned attack with the purpose of bringing home the Spanish treasure fleet.

Six ships would sail under Lord Thomas Howard, the nephew of the Lord Admiral. Reluctantly Elizabeth yielded to everyone's pleading and appointed Walter vice-admiral. It was his first high naval command and he was exultant. All winter he worked tirelessly on the preparations, and then in the spring of 1591, when they were ready to sail, the queen once more refused to let him go. He was forced to hand over his command to Richard Grenville. Not even her promise of a splendid country home in Dorset made up for the keen disappointment.

All that summer he chafed against the bonds that tied him to the court while the others were on the high seas. Then there was Bess. He was thirty-seven. He wanted a wife and children. Earlier in the year, when Robert Cecil had met Elizabeth Brooke, the little man had been very unhappy. He had asked Walter if any pretty girl could possibly fall in love with such a wretched hunchback as himself and Walter had assured him that true love takes little notice of looks. Now Robert was happily married, and the queen had raised no objection. But Walter's case was quite different. All he had was the gift of Elizabeth. If he dared to reveal how much he loved Bess, she might strip him of everything he possessed. The memory of her treatment of Essex, or of other men who were not nearly as close to her as himself, was far too vivid. On that one point, no one was able to move her. He could see no way out of his dilemma, so he hesitated and continued to meet Bess in secret.

Meanwhile, there came calamitous news from the fleet. The squadron waiting off the Azores for Spanish treasure ships had been attacked while desperately unprepared. Lord Thomas Howard had succeeded in forcing his way through, but Richard Grenville stopped to pick up his sick men off the island of Flores and then with daredevil gallantry decided on cutting his way through the Spanish fleet. His rash action might have succeeded if the wind had not failed and left him becalmed under the lee of a towering ship.

Walter was divided between exasperation at Grenville's lack of discipline and admiration of his courage. When the queen, who never had any patience with heroism that did not bring some practical advantage, spoke harshly of Grenville's recklessness, he defended his cousin with passion.

"Would you have acted in the same way, Walter?" she asked him coolly.

He hesitated. "There was another course, Your Majesty, but in the greatness of his heart he would not let himself be persuaded to it. The *Revenge* fought for fifteen hours, fifty-three men-of-war were not able to take her, and when Sir Richard was mortally wounded, he commanded his master gunner to split and sink the ship rather than dishonor himself and his country by surrendering to the enemy."

"Sir Richard would have carried the lives of a great number

of my good seamen with him," commented the queen dryly. "I thank God he was prevented from such a foolhardy deed."

She was right, as she nearly always was, but it helped to distract Walter's mind to write the story of the last glorious battle of the *Revenge*. He hoped it would shut the mouths of the critics who slandered Sir Richard's heroic folly now that he was dead and could not defend himself. The brilliance of the style and the vivid word pictures he drew in the *Report of the Truth of the Fight about the Azores* has stirred the imagination of poets and historians ever since. It was the first of his writings to be printed under his own name. In earlier years, when a publisher had dared to publish some of his very personal poems without his consent, he had angrily demanded that every copy should be withdrawn and his name blotted out.

On November 19 Arthur Throckmorton came back from a visit to Paris and noted in his diary the astounding news he heard from his sister. Early in the autumn Walter had come to an important decision. He and Bess had been quietly married, only their closest friends admitted to the secret. Then, undaunted by Grenville's death and the loss of the *Revenge*, he began to plan a new expedition to capture the silver fleet and sack Panama. This time he persuaded the queen to allow him to lead it himself. He was determined to bring back so much treasure that she would find it impossible not to forgive him when he broke the news of his marriage. He had forgotten that the whim of fortune can be as fickle as the wind and weather at sea.

8 : *"True Love is a durable Fire"*

—Walter Ralegh

Walter was at the Chatham dockyards busy with final preparations for his new expedition when a messenger arrived with the news. Bess had borne him a son in her brother's house in London. In his joy he would have liked to drop everything and ride back to her, but he did not dare. Rumors of his marriage were cropping up everywhere and already he had been forced to lie desperately to Robert Cecil.

The coming of the baby had been added worry. It had not been easy for Bess to hide her pregnancy from the other girls at court, but no one had guessed. Early in the year she obtained permission to visit her brother, but if their secret were to be kept, she must part with their little son and return to her duties. The baby must be cared for by relatives. No word of their marriage had yet reached the queen, and the sooner Walter was at sea and out of her reach, the better.

The ships set out from Falmouth in Cornwall, the sails white as seabirds in the May sunshine. Walter led them in *Roebuck*. Within a few days, Martin Frobisher overtook him with a message from Elizabeth commanding him to return to her immediately. This was not unlike what she had done in the past, but for the first time he defied her direct order and sailed on for another week. The Portuguese merchantmen laden with all the wealth of the East Indies would soon be making for Lisbon. The prize was almost within his grasp. It was maddening to be forced to hand over his command to Frobisher, who was a good seaman but too strict with the men. They feared and disliked him as much as they loved Walter, and Walter felt increasingly worried about this venture on which he had recklessly staked not only his future but almost every penny he possessed.

Before he landed at Plymouth, the news of his marriage had at last been brought to Elizabeth, and she was filled with a royal rage at his deception. She had given him princely gifts. He had been as close to her as a lover. The devotion he had poured out in fine verses was all a lie. He had dared to reject her for one of her own maids of honor. Bitter tears of humiliation stung her eyes. At that moment she could willingly have sent them both to death—but Elizabeth was no tyrant. If he humbled himself, if he threw himself at her feet pleading for mercy, she might relent a little.

The whole court was humming with the scandal. He had been so sure of himself, so proudly different from others, and now he had been caught out like everyone else. They looked forward eagerly to his disgrace. It was not long in coming. Still not aware that his secret had been discovered, Walter came back and even before he went to court had his little son brought to him at Durham House. Then the blow fell.

The queen had waited long enough for him to confess his crime. Bess was dismissed from court; Walter was confined to his own house and George Carew was put in charge of him. It was the most unpleasant duty George had ever undertaken. Walter would not accept it calmly. He had always been certain that when the moment came, he would be able to charm the queen into forgiveness as he had done so often for others. Now he was forbidden to approach her.

Walter had been imprisoned for a nerve-racking month when Arthur Gorges called one day to cheer him up. George shook his head at him hopelessly while Walter stared moodily out of his study window. Suddenly Walter swung around, his eyes alive with excitement.

"The queen's barge is coming upriver from Blackfriars. My boatman will row me across the Thames. If I can see her . . . only for a moment . . ."

"It is impossible," said George Carew firmly.

"Do you want to break my heart?" exclaimed Walter wildly. "You shall not prevent me. My enemies shall not have it all their own way. I will take a boat. I will row myself. . . ."

His cousin stood resolutely between him and the door, and Walter hurled himself at him. They struggled together and, maddened by the resistance, Walter drew his dagger. Arthur Gorges, realizing that he was in earnest, tried to separate them and the blade slashed across his knuckles. The sight of the blood brought Walter to his senses. He threw down his dagger and walked away from them with a feeling of despair.

All his efforts to reach the queen were useless. A week later she sent him to prison.

The Tower of London was an ancient fortress, both palace

and prison, on the banks of the Thames. The central tower had been begun by William the Conqueror. For centuries traitors had been imprisoned in its dank and evil-smelling dungeons. They had been racked and tortured within and beheaded on Tower Green. But there were more attractive apartments, where Elizabeth had stayed for a few days before her coronation, where the lieutenant governor had his lodgings. There was a mint, and ammunition was stored there for use in time of war. There was a menagerie with six magnificent lions and the famous ravens with their allowance of twopence a day for meat. If they ever flew away, said an old tradition, then the Tower would crumble and England's glory would vanish forever.

Walter was not treated harshly. He had a comfortable room. He was allowed books, writing materials, and a servant to attend on him, but he was not permitted to see Bess, though she was in the same building and he was tormented with anxiety about his future. He worried particularly about Bess, who apart from her brother had no one but himself to care for her.

"My heart was never broken till this day," he wrote to Robert Cecil, "when I hear the queen goes away so far off whom I have followed so many years with so great love . . . and am now left behind her in a dark prison all alone."

As he had done so often when alone and unhappy, Walter turned to poetry. Unable to plead with the queen personally, he would pour out his grief to her in his verses.

The Book of the Ocean to Cynthia, he called it. "Water," "Ocean" had always been her playful names for him. He wrote of his years of devotion, and despite his desire to please her, could not prevent bitterness creeping in. Never once had she let him do what he had wanted more than anything else. He had been no more than her slave. Even on this last voyage . . . His pen flew angrily across the page:

> When I was gone, she sent her memory
> More strong than were ten thousand ships of war
> To call me back, to leave great honour's thought
> To leave my friends, my fortune, my attempt,
> To leave the purpose I so long had sought . . .

The poem was never finished, never even revised. He heard in his cell that the expedition he had planned made the capture he had hoped for. Off the Azores, the *Roebuck* took the great East Indian ship *Madre de Dios*, with an enormous cargo of gold and jewels, of spices, of amber and ebony, of silks, damasks, and tapestries. It was the largest and richest ship ever to be captured by Englishmen.

When it was towed into Dartmouth, the whole West Country went crazy with excitement. The seamen, rebellious and angry that Walter had been imprisoned, mutinied against their unpopular captains. They pillaged and looted where they could, making off with bags of rubies and diamonds and gold cups, with spices and perfumes, until there was scarcely a cottage in Devon that did not smell as sweet as a palace.

The docks were like Saint Bartholomew's Fair, wrote a contemporary, with merchants, tradesmen, thieves, and beggars pushing their way in and fighting for a share of the plunder. The Privy Council were in despair. Robert Cecil hurried down to Dartmouth and was met by John Hawkins and John Gilbert, two extremely worried men, trying to deal with a hopeless situation.

"There is one especial man who could settle this confusion in a trice," said John Hawkins crisply, "and the Queen's Grace keeps him locked up in the Tower!"

So Walter was released and rode down to Devon under guard to such a welcome that Robert Cecil was both astonished and upset. His own authority meant nothing beside that of the prisoner. The captains and seamen crowded around him, congratulating him, clapping him on the shoulder, shaking him by the hand, though Walter was careful to say again and again, "You are mistaken, my friends. I am still the queen's poor captive."

By working early and late he saved most of the cargo, and he made up his mind that when it was all settled, he was not going back to prison.

"Fourscore thousand pounds is more than ever a man presented to Her Majesty," he wrote to the Lord Treasurer with a touch of pride. "If God has sent it for my ransom, I hope Her Majesty will accept it."

It was he who had suffered loss. He had planned the expedition, invested more money than anyone, done all the hard work, and come off the worst. But at least he was free. Just before Christmas, Bess was released from the Tower. For six months they had been separated. Now at last he could take his bride to his new home in Dorset. But sorrow went with them. The baby whose coming had caused so much anxiety had died during the summer.

In the spring of 1593 Walter set about repairing his Norman castle at Sherborne. It had three great towers, a moat, and a drawbridge, but it was old-fashioned, uncomfortable, and very cold. After a few months he decided to build a new modern house for Bess on a little rise overlooking the river. Sherborne was a lovely spot, green and fertile. In the gardens he planted fruit trees—peach, nectarine, black cherries, and apricots. As well as the damask roses and the clove pinks, there were sunflowers from Peru, nasturtiums from America, lilies from Turkey, and the lilac and wallflowers he had grown in Ireland.

"*True Love is a durable Fire*" : 97

Although he was banished from the court, the queen had not taken any of his offices from him. His abilities were far too great to be left unused. He was still powerful in Devon and Cornwall. He was still Captain of the Guard, too, though since he was forbidden to enter the queen's presence, he had to appoint a deputy.

During the summer his friends began to gather around him once more—Tom Hariot, Lawrence Keymis, the eccentric Earl of Northumberland, the poet George Chapman. His wife welcomed them at Sherborne and they became her friends too. Bess was expecting another baby. She would sit with them in Walter's study, stitching at some little garment, while the talk went on and on. She was not learned, and much of it flew high above her head, but she saw how Walter led the discussion, how he enjoyed a keen argument, how eagerly they all listened to him. It made her realize how difficult it was for him to adapt himself to the slow ways of their country neighbors, to whom he was a brilliant stranger, too clever, too proud and ambitious and outspoken to be reliable or popular.

Everything worked against him in the shadow of his disgrace. Up in London, Christopher Marlowe was killed in a sordid tavern brawl and it stirred up the old scandals about his atheism among the circle that had met at Durham House. A young playwright called Will Shakespeare, greatly favored by Essex and his new friend the Earl of Southampton, was busy writing a play that made fun of the "School of Night," as they had now begun to call Walter's intellectual group of friends. The young courtiers laughed themselves into stitches at *Love's Labour's Lost*, with the fantastical Don Armado, a malicious caricature in which the actor mimicked Walter to the very life. He treated it with contempt, but twisted inwardly at the mockery.

Walter's second son was born in October. Wat was a sturdy, dark-haired baby, the image of his father, and from the very start he was indulged and spoiled by his parents. Bess hoped that now her husband would settle down contentedly into their quiet country life, but she was no sooner up and about again than she realized that something new was being planned. She would come into a room to find Walter and Tom Hariot bent over charts and maps spread out on the table. His attempt to colonize Virginia had failed. Now he was determined to try something different. Spain had occupied Mexico and Panama. They had penetrated South America, but only in the northwest, where Pizarro had conquered Peru. There were still other parts to be explored.

"Why has this Guiana so captured your interest?" asked Hariot.

"There are so many reasons. It is a land open to our conquest, for one thing. Then the rumors of gold to be found there are too many and too well authenticated to be ignored. But there is far more than that. The Spaniards have ventured there time and time again, but only to rob and murder the Indians. If I can persuade their chiefs to accept us as allies, we could establish it as an overseas dominion that could give to England the riches that Spain obtains from Peru."

It was the old dream of empire that had possessed him for so long. Hariot said, "Do you see yourself as another Pizarro?"

"He destroyed the Inca civilization. I want to take the Indians under England's protection." Walter was pacing up and down the room, his eyes alight with enthusiasm. "There is nothing written about Guiana that I have not read. El Dorado! The golden man! Do you know, Tom, that Johannes Martinez wrote that at the Inca's great feasts in the city of Manoa, all those swearing loyalty to him were stripped naked, smeared with balsam, and covered in gold dust so that they shone from head to foot like statues of gold."

"Manoa!" murmured Hariot, raising his eyebrows. "Do you really believe in it?"

"You may smile, Tom, but is it not at least possible that the last Inca fleeing from Pizarro after he had murdered Atahualpa found his way to the mountains of Guiana and set up his kingdom there?"

"Do you hope to establish a colony?"

"One day, perhaps. Now I have not sufficient money. Since my disgrace, there are few willing to invest in my trading voyages. My ships have been lying idle. I shall be hard put to find enough cash to finance an expedition without selling some of my estates. But at least I can send Jacob Whiddon to spy out the land. He is one of my most reliable captains." He bent over the map again. "It would appear that the river Orinoco reaches the sea in a kind of delta. The city of Manoa, if it exists, must be hundreds of miles upstream."

Bess felt a cold shiver run through her. He would be sailing up an unknown river into unimaginable dangers with enemies lurking behind every tree. Yet she knew only too well that if he had set his heart on it, not all her pleading would hold him back.

9 : "The great rich and beautiful empire of Guiana"

—Walter Ralegh

"Try some of these oysters, gentlemen. They are salty but they have a fine crusty flavor," said Walter, leaning back in his carved ebony chair and looking around at the guests he was feasting in his luxurious cabin. Keymis sat at his right hand, next to Captain Whiddon, whose favorable report had helped Walter decide to sail to South America. Then there was Humphrey's son, John Gilbert, and Richard Grenville's second boy. There had been no lack of adventurous young gentlemen eager to sail with him to Guiana.

He had left Plymouth in February 1595. The previous year had been full of trouble. The death of his mother had taken him to Exeter to bury her beside his father and settle her affairs. Danger of Spanish invasion on the Cornish coast had sent him to sea with Admiral Howard, where he could not sleep for anx-

"The great rich and beautiful empire of Guiana" : 101

iety about the plague, which had crept out of London as far as Sherborne. "My Bess is on one way sent; her son, another way; and I am in great trouble therewith," he wrote to a friend.

At last everything was ready and Bess had come down to Devon to see him off, trying hard to keep back the tears as she checked every item in his cabin, the bed with its gilded dolphin feet and green silk hangings and the brass-bound chest overflowing with books to read during the long days at sea. Little Wat had screamed in temper when she had taken him from his father's arms before they said goodbye and were rowed ashore.

Walter had left a foggy wintry England behind him and sailed into a new world of sunlit seas, where the flying fish rose out of the foam around the prow and the laughing dolphins rolled over one another in the ship's wake. Now it was April and already he had been exploring along the Guiana shore.

"It is a remarkable sight," he explained to his guests. "The oysters hang like sea fruit in the roots of the mangrove trees as they thrust down toward the seabed. I plucked them myself."

He had spent the evening outlining his plans and making his intentions absolutely clear to his young companions. "We shall not take so much as a potato root from the Indians without payment, and if any one of the men, no matter who he is, robs one of them or harms the women, I swear he shall hang for it."

"You will find it impatient work with some of the meaner sort," remarked Keymis.

"Maybe, but my mind is made up. No Christian nation has the right to invade and murder primitive peoples simply because they are heathen." They gaped at him in surprise, and impatience rose in him because they could not understand that no true commonwealth of nations could be built on blood and the sword. Walter was determined to win the friendship of the natives by kindness, in contrast to the cruelty of the Spaniards.

When they had landed and captured the settlement of San José, in Trinidad, he had been horrified at what he had seen: women burned and tortured; men hung with chains that ate into their living flesh; others tied back to back and left to starve in the jungle. He had released them himself and mercifully killed those beyond help.

He took prisoner the Spanish governor, Antonio de Berreo, and astonished the old man by treating him with a fine courtesy. They dined together on the best of his food and wine while Walter wormed out of him all the information he could. Manoa, that fabulous city which the Spaniards had sought in vain, seemed to hover tantalizingly before his fascinated eyes. It was said to be so large that it took a day and a half to walk from the gate to the emperor's palace, and the gardens were crowded with figures of birds and beasts and flowers all in pure gold. El Dorado! The magic words were tossed from one to the other among the men on the lower decks. But in the meantime they had reached Trinidad and there were more practical problems to be solved.

Walter called together the chiefs of the coastal tribes, telling them that he served a powerful and noble queen who would deliver them from the cruel oppression of Spain and take them under her protection. Then he pulled out the gold chain he wore under his collar and showed them the jeweled miniature that hung from it. In a hushed silence they passed Elizabeth's portrait from one hand to the other, gazing with awe at the white face, the red-gold hair curling like little serpents, the transparent ruff standing out like wings. Was she a goddess, they whispered, and falling on their knees would have worshipped if he had not prevented them.

After that, the Indians gave willing help and Walter made ready for the great adventure. One hundred men were packed

The New York Public Library Picture Collection

Sir Walter during the siege of San José, Trinidad. Engraving by Theodore de Bry

into five small boats. They were unprotected from torrential rain or burning sun, and they cooked, ate, and slept on the hard boards. With the men's unwashed bodies and wet clothes, the intense heat of the sun and the constant smell of cooking fish, conditions were more loathesome than in an English prison, as wrote Walter feelingly in the journal he had begun to keep.

For days they wandered, hopelessly lost, in the great tangle of waters at the mouth of the Orinoco, but at last their Indian guide turned into the right channel and they went up the river on the flood tide, only to stick fast on a sandbank. It was a miracle that their venture did not end there and then, with the boats immovable and half the men perched like rooks in the trees. But with much hauling and pulling and casting all but the barest necessities overboard, they dragged themselves free and went on.

The flood of the river had slackened and they had to pull harder at the oars. Walter instituted hourly turns of rowing, gentlemen taking a share right along with everyone else.

Day followed day as their boats glided through green tunnels, the giant creepers looping from the tall trees and tangling across the water in front of them. On either side, myriads of birds—carnation, blue, crimson, orange-tawny, and purple—flitted through the branches like jewels. They passed a settlement where the natives built their houses on stilts and moved them higher as the floodwater rose. They shivered when their Indian guide mumbled in his broken Spanish of a people whose heads grew beneath their shoulders and of a savage tribe whose women went to war instead of their men. The tales helped to pass the time, but their food was beginning to run short. There was no bread left, and though they plucked the fruits growing along the banks and shot an occasional bird, they grew faint with hunger.

The sun burned down relentlessly and thirst tormented them, for there was nothing to drink but the thick, slimy river water.

Walter went from one man to another, encouraging them, jesting, and trying to make light of their misery. "Only a few hours more—maybe one more day—and I swear we will reach a settlement where you will eat to bursting. Would you be called fainthearts? If we return now, we shall surely starve by the way and the world will laugh us to scorn."

They were almost at their last gasp when the old Indian guide assured them that if they took a branch to the right he would bring them soon to a place where there was food in abundance. The channel was so narrow that Walter took only the smallest of the boats and a few men. They set out early in the morning, but after three hours' hard rowing, there was no sign of a village.

"A little farther, my lord, only a little farther," pleaded the Indian, but they rowed on all the hours of the day, and still there was nothing. They had taken no food with them and eaten little before they set out. It was dark as pitch by now, and the way was so narrow they had to cut their way through the branches of the trees with their swords.

"Hang the traitor," cried the men, hunger gnawing at their stomachs. "He has betrayed us and we shall surely die."

The old man screamed in terror, but Walter restrained the men; and his trust in the Indian was justified. At one o'clock in the morning, after seventeen hours of nightmare, they saw a faint glimmer of light and heard the frenzied barking of village dogs. In the chief's house they feasted on baked fish and roasted chickens. They ate fresh baked bread and drank a strong Indian drink flavored with pepper and herbs. They rested there for a few hours and in the morning, their boats laden with provisions, they returned to their comrades, who welcomed them with thankfulness, for they had believed them all dead.

"Let us go on," cried the men joyfully, their courage renewed. "We care not how far!"

Up the river they rowed by grassy plains where the deer came down to feed at the water's side. Their surroundings were so beautiful that they forgot the menaces lurking in the shallows until a young man in their company leaped laughing into the cool water and was seized and devoured by alligators before their very eyes.

When they arrived at the little port of Morequito, Walter had a tent set up and sent an Indian runner for the great king of all the tribes. Topiawari came the next day with his wives and children, bringing them gifts of fine fish, venison, pork, chickens, baskets of juicy mangoes, and the delicious pineapples that Walter called the "princess of fruits."

The simplicity and noble dignity of the old chieftain, whom those in England would regard as no more than a savage, impressed Walter deeply. They spoke together all the day, helped out by the interpreter and the chief's meager Spanish.

"You have treated my people with justice and liberality, my lord," he said gravely. "I would willingly give you guides and food, but you cannot reach the city of Manoa in this season. It is many days' journey into the blue mountains and soon the rains will come, the rivers will overflow, and the paths disappear. You would perish on your way."

"But it does exist, Topiawari," Walter insisted, trying to read the truth behind the old man's sunken eyes. "That's what I would know. That it is there, however difficult the search."

"In my father's time, my lord, there came down a people from as far off as where the sun sleeps, their garments strange and red as the wood that supports your tent, and they told me of the great city and the Inca's palace where even the dishes on his tables and in his kitchens were of gold and silver."

Manoa was like a mirage, sometimes seeming real and sometimes insubstantial as a dream.

"It is not only the gold I look for," Walter went on, "but to conquer this lost kingdom so that all this land can be united in one dominion with my country."

"I have seen many come and go, my lord, but none whose dream would reach so far. I am an old man—more than a hundred winters have whitened my hair, and every day I am called for by death. When you return, send to me again and I will come to you."

When they pushed out their boats in the early morning, the mist was thick as curdled milk, but presently the sky cleared to sapphire, and higher up where the Orinoco reached the Caroni, there were great waterfalls that rose one above the other higher than a church tower and fell with the sound of a thousand clashing bells. With their daggers they dug out of the rocks glittering stones, which Walter judged to be marcasite. They would have explored farther but for the storms. The rain made it impossible to delay if they were to reach their ships before the river flooded.

Back in Morequito, Walter waited for Topiawari while the Indians packed the boats with provisions. Night after night, when he scribbled in his journal, the beauty of the country haunted him.

"It was all fair green grass," he wrote. "The deer crossing in every path, the birds toward the evening singing on every tree with a thousand several tunes; cranes and herons of white, crimson, and carnation perching on the river's side, and the air fresh with a gentle easterly wind."

When Topiawari came, Walter spoke with him again, promising to return the following year with a larger force that would protect the Indians against Spain and would go on to Manoa. The old chief begged him to take his son with him to England.

"Let him learn of your country," he said, "so that when I am called to my ancestors, he may be king here in my place, and when you come again, there may be friendship between your land and mine."

When Walter embarked, the natives crowded around him, piling gifts into the boats, kissing his hands, imploring him to return. He was touched by their simplicity and their belief in him. He would keep his promise if it were humanly possible. As their boats shot down the river, he saw them wading into the water, swimming after them to wave farewell.

The journey back to the ships was dark and stormy. They were soaked through to the skin ten times a day. The Orinoco overflowed its banks, its current so fast it carried them sometimes a hundred miles in a day. When they reached the delta, they were in desperate straits. The thunder and lightning, the winds and the heavy rains lashed the sea to tempest, and every moment they feared the swamping of their small boats. By midnight, as soon as the storm had lessened a little, Walter took the lead and they crept across the dark heaving waters, until thankfully they saw the lanterns of their ships anchored near Trinidad.

Safely back in his cabin once again, Walter was not dissatisfied. He had successfully mapped some six hundred miles of unknown country; he was carrying back samples of ore that surely contained gold; Keymis had returned from an excursion of his own with news of a gold mine not far from their route. The men had behaved well and only one life had been lost.

Now all he had to do was to persuade the queen that his long-cherished dream of an English empire rivaling that of Spain could become a reality. He began to turn his journal into a narrative, one copy to go to her, another to Robert Cecil. Surely she could not fail to see, as he could, the enormous untapped resources of this beautiful country.

The journey home was uneventful and passed quickly.

It was good finally to be back at Sherborne with all its home comforts, to kiss his wife and toss his son in his arms. The tottering baby he remembered was a sturdy two-year-old, full of mischief, running everywhere.

His book was published and was an instant success. The first edition sold out at once. Whatever the public thought of the author, that dark figure with so many dangerous ideas, they were enthralled by the vivid picture he had drawn of a strange and wonderful country. But his real purpose achieved nothing at all.

In the months away he had forgotten the hostility he had left behind him. Essex and his young friends were openly contemptuous. Whoever had heard of oysters that grew in trees or men who lived in treetops? He was nothing but a liar, a cheat, a coward who had not been to Guiana at all but had skulked in Cornwall and let other men brave the dangers for him. The mockery of men who had never stirred a step out of their own country infuriated him, but none of it would have mattered if only he could have convinced Elizabeth. Forbidden her presence, how could he make her see Guiana as he did? He stressed the gold in the ore he had brought back, but there was far more in his mind than that. An advanced country like England, he wrote, should not conquer a primitive land with the sword but be its partner, sending technicians and advisers rather than soldiers, developing it, bringing its young men back to England to be educated so that they could lead their people to practice Christianity and the arts of civilization.

Tom Hariot was hard at work designing a map with all the discoveries clearly marked. George Chapman burst into verse:

Riches and conquest and renown I sing,
Riches with honour, conquest without blood,
Enough to seat the Monarchy of Earth
Like to Jove's eagle on Eliza's hand.

But Walter's proposals received no encouragement. Lord Burghley had never had any patience with his vision of empire. Cecil studied his arguments and dismissed them as impractical. Elizabeth read his book with interest but could see no immediate gain for herself. He is a poet still, she thought, and for a moment her heart was stirred, but he had preferred Elizabeth Throckmorton to Elizabeth Tudor and he could go on making the best of his choice.

Walter suffered the penalty of those whose minds outrun their own time, and there was nothing he could do. In the New Year he sent Keymis to Guiana to maintain the contact he had been at such pains to establish, and threw himself into life at Sherborne. From the castle windows, the pale golden stone of his new house could be glimpsed through the trees. He worked on his gardens and extended his estates; he rode out hawking and hunting with his neighbors; he thought of writing some kind of historical work and filled a notebook with ideas. None of it was sufficient to occupy his tireless energy and he indulged in an orgy of scientific experiments with Northumberland, Hariot, and anyone else interested. His reputation suffered among the ignorant country folk, and even when Bess urged him not to encourage such damaging gossip, he was bitterly contemptuous.

10 : *"Now all the youth of England are on fire"*

—William Shakespeare

At long last the queen had need of Walter. She still refused to see him, but in March of 1596 he was called to a council of war. While he had been in Guiana, Spain had dared to invade Cornwall, burning and killing along the coast. It was time to teach King Philip another sharp lesson.

"We must attack Cadiz," said Walter boldly. "I said it years ago, before the Armada, and I say it again. Cadiz is their naval base. Destroy it and we will have plucked the heart from their enterprise."

They were gathered around the council table, the young Earl of Essex, the gray-haired Lord Admiral, his nephew Lord Thomas Howard, George Carew, who had been made Master of the Ordnance and controlled the artillery.

"Cadiz," objected the admiral. "It is too dangerous. We would be walking into the enemy's jaws."

"The Spanish have a proverb, my lord. 'The lion is not so fierce as he is painted.' Our ships and guns are second to none. Let us show them our power, not sit meekly on defense waiting for them to ravage our land."

The audacity of the plan appealed to Essex. He was ready to forget his hostility to Walter in this purpose, for he was eager to win fame in some fine military exploit. They would sail in June, Essex as commander of the land army, and Admiral Howard and his nephew in charge at sea, while Walter controlled a squadron as rear admiral.

All that soakingly wet April and May, he was riding up and down the lanes of Kent, personally recruiting seamen and hunting after runaway mariners. "As far as we press men one day, they come away another and say they will not serve," he wrote to Robert Cecil on a dirty scrap of paper in a filthy tavern. It was always difficult to find crews for the hard and dangerous life on board a warship.

Bess's brother, Arthur, was going with him. She came to London to stay in his house and be with Walter, but she saw very little of her husband. He would ride in at evening tired, wet, his boots mud-splashed to the thighs, longing only for dry clothes and decent food. He would kiss her hurriedly, pat little Wat on the head, and then be off again. It was only a few months since he had come back from Guiana, and now he would be going into all the danger and fury of war. Sometimes she wished she was like Lady Cecil, who always had Robert by her side. But then Lady Cecil's little boy, Will, was a sickly child, not at all like her lively Wat.

The crews were gathered and the expedition got under way at last. Walter's *Warspite* led his squadron into the Bay of San

Sebastian just outside Cadiz after a scorching June day spent scouring the coast for enemy ships on the run. He could not believe the scene of confusion that met his eyes.

The fleet was to have been the spearhead. It would sail into the harbor to make a massed attack on the enemy defenses, and only when that was successful would the army go on to the taking of the town. Now it was obvious that Essex's soldiers were being embarked for invasion. A strong wind had whipped up the sea, the overloaded boats were already sinking, men were struggling in the water, the ships were out of formation. It was an indescribably hopeless muddle.

He was so angry at the stupidity that was going to wreck the whole enterprise that he dropped into his skiff and was rowed across to *Repulse* in a white heat of rage. Essex received him coldly and Walter found it impossible to control his temper.

"More than half your men will be drowned before ever they reach the shore, my lord," he was shouting as he climbed up the rope they dropped down to him. "Do you think to capture Cadiz with a seasick rabble?"

"I cannot now withdraw my troops and keep my honor," replied the earl obstinately.

"By God," exclaimed Walter, "do you talk of honor when at one throw you are casting away Her Majesty's safety and our country's future?"

"It was the Lord Admiral's decision," replied Essex, glad to put the blame on someone else. "He will not consent to risk his ships until the town is taken."

"Will you allow me to speak to him myself?"

Essex was not sorry to shift responsibility. He watched anxiously as Walter's skiff scudded across the rough water, the spray breaking over it.

Admiral Howard listened to his rear admiral, where he had

ignored the young earl, and with a touch of generosity agreed to Walter's pleading that he should be allowed to lead the attack himself.

As his skiff skimmed past *Repulse* on his way back to *Warspite*, Walter stood up in the dangerously rocking boat. "*Entramos*," he shouted in Spanish. "In we go!" and his exultant wave nearly sent him overboard, while Essex cheered and tossed his jeweled cap into the sea like a schoolboy.

There were not many hours of daylight left to collect the men back into the ships and discuss the plan of battle. It was ten at night before Walter had written his orders of attack and they had been dispatched to each commander.

He had no thought of rest. At peep of day he weighed anchor and led his squadron, *Warspite* and *Mary Rose*, *Dreadnought*, *Lion*, *Rainbow*, and *Swiftsure*, into the narrow channel under close fire from the shore batteries, his trumpets blaring contemptuously. The galleys guarding the entrance took to their oars in terror and the great galleons under their apostolic leaders, the *St. Philip* and the *St. Andrew*, *St. Thomas* and *St. Matthew*, moved majestically against him. He pulled up alongside the *St. Philip*, the thought racing through his mind that today he would exact vengeance for Richard Grenville and the loss of the *Revenge*.

To the Spanish sailors in the heat and rage of the day, the tall lean figure of the English admiral in his black corselet glimpsed here and there in the dense smoke of the gunfire seemed like a demon of destruction. By afternoon he realized that he must board the *St. Philip* or be sunk, but the risk was great without the help of the small flyboats, which were unable to force their way up the choked channel.

Anxiously he dropped into his skiff once again and consulted

"Now all the youth of England are on fire" : 115

with Essex, all enmity forgotten in the heat of the battle. Impulsively the earl cried, "We must not fail now. Board her if needs be. I swear I will back you to the hilt."

Back on his own ship, Walter found that *Nonpareil* and *Rainbow* had pushed ahead. He nosed between them and drew across the channel. No one was going to rob him of his opportunity. Today he would win glory or die in the attempt.

He warped alongside the huge galleon, and to the shrill screaming of pipes, the men swarmed onto the deck. Like rats, the Spaniards fled before the English sailors, tumbling over the side like coals poured from a sack. The great ship heeled over on the mudbank, there was a towering sheet of flame as the gunpowder store caught fire, and a wave of heat that almost stopped one's breath. Through the billows of black smoke, he saw men running, screaming, leaping from the poop, hanging by ropes, swimming desperately with great wounds, a sight terrible as hell itself.

The *St. Thomas* was in flames, the *St. Matthew* and the *St. Andrew* yielding, the Spanish admiral from the *St. Philip* preparing to surrender, when Walter staggered and fell against the ship's rail. He would have rolled into the sea if his sailors had not caught him. A chance bullet had bounced up from the deck and struck him in the thigh, splinters from the wooden planking lacerating the wound horribly.

The Spanish commander was coming on board. Walter received his submission with a few words of courtesy in his own tongue before fainting.

Down in the cockpit, among the dead and the dying, the ship's surgeon began to cut away the cloth embedded in the wound, Walter still giving orders to his ship's master.

"One more thing, Captain Davis," he called after him as he

hurried away. "Send out the longboats and pick up as many of those poor half-burned devils as you can."

Walter shuddered at the touch of the forceps withdrawing the splinters and the feel of the long iron probe searching into the wound for the musket ball. But there was little time to rest his wounded leg. All night the small boats raced between the ships, carrying messages to plan the next day's campaign.

In the brilliant early-morning sunlight, the troops were landed for the capture of the town. The Spanish had sent out a body of cavalry in opposition, but the victory at sea had demoralized them. They retreated before the violent assault of the English and fled, some to the bridge that led into the town, others leaping down a low wall that opened into the suburbs.

After his exhausting night, Walter had himself carried ashore and rode beside Essex at the head of the victorious army, but the pain of his wound was too great. He had not slept for more than two days and his head swam with fatigue and fever. The Lord Admiral ordered him back to the ship, since in any case no one had been left in charge of the fleet.

He could not lie quietly in his cabin and do nothing. He sent Arthur Throckmorton ashore at dawn next day to ask permission to capture the Spanish merchant ships lying tantalizingly in Puerto Reale harbor loaded with valuable cargoes. Essex, flushed with success, bestowing knighthoods on his followers like a conquering prince, and merrily plundering the captured city, was far too busy to send back the men he would need. The Duke of Medina Sidonia, who for years had smarted under the shame of the Armada defeat, emptied the ships of everything of value and burned them before Walter's infuriated eyes.

There were bitter arguments when Essex returned and realized his mistake. The queen would think little of the glory of victory but a great deal of the loss of the treasure that would pay her troops. In a rage of temper he put the blame on Walter, accusing him of negligence.

Sick and feverish from his wound, Walter replied angrily, resenting the injustice. The friendship they had found in the heat of battle was destroyed.

Trying to remedy the loss, Essex suggested that they should wait for the Mexican silver fleet. "It is due any day now," he said confidently.

"You are no seaman, my lord," retorted Walter, "or you would realize the folly of such a suggestion. Our ships are battered, our men weary, our food is running short. To fight another battle would be to court disaster."

This time the Lord Admiral had the last word. He had no intention of risking the queen's valuable ships in any such harebrained scheme. They must be content with their present victory.

The Spanish knew who was responsible for the English victory. In his dark windowless room in the Escorial, the Spanish king looked down at the names of the English pirates who had troubled him for so many years. His pen struck them out one by one—Richard Grenville was long gone; Martin Frobisher had died of wounds a year before; Drake and John Hawkins had been buried at sea on their last tragic voyage—but there was still another name and he underlined it with heavy black strokes. The score against "Guatteral," as the Spanish called Walter, was steadily growing—all those captured merchantmen, the Armada, Guiana, and now Cadiz. One day there would come a reckoning.

While King Philip painstakingly counted up his losses and, undaunted, made plans for a new assault, Elizabeth was in a royal rage with her commanders.

"By God's son, what return have you brought me for my fifty thousand pounds? Nothing but crippled ships and a demand for the seamen's pay."

Essex flushed and muttered something. She turned a crushing look on him, angry with herself because she still loved his handsome, boyish face. "As for you, my lord," she went on, "do not imagine that I am impressed by the people shouting for you in the streets. You have handed out my honors to your favorites like so many cheap prizes at a fair. You have made knighthood something for children to laugh at!"

Every grocer's apprentice was singing a mocking ballad about the knights of Cadiz, but Essex was the national hero. The common people gave scarce a thought to Walter. Only Elizabeth and those closest to her knew to whom the victory was really due. George Carew had written glowingly of his cousin; even from one of Essex's closest supporters had come words of praise.

"Sir Walter Ralegh did (in my judgment) no man better. . . . I never knew the gentleman before this time; and I am sorry for it, for there are in him excellent things beside his valor."

Walter had spent some months at Sherborne slowly recovering from his wound. He knew now that he would limp for the rest of his days, but for the first time since the queen had forced him into obscurity, he was more content with his life. He had not forgotten his promise to return to Guiana, but since the war with Spain was still an ever-present anxiety, he could obtain no official support. Keymis had returned reporting that the Indians spoke of him with affection and that he had information of another gold mine. All Walter could do to keep the contact alive was to send one of his captains with his new ship, christened the *Wat* as a birthday gift for his son. That winter he pursued another project with some success.

Rumors had been spreading of the new Armada Philip was gathering together. Walter urged that once again they should take the offensive and go into attack, repeating the success of Cadiz. Essex was on fire at the very idea. Unexpectedly he and Walter drew very close.

"We shall render his most Catholic Majesty a king of figs and oranges as he was in olden days," said Walter gaily at one of the many talks they had together, swinging the ebony cane his wound had forced him to carry. Essex laughed and clapped him enthusiastically on the shoulder. In some moods the earl could be charming, impulsively generous, and chivalrous. It was the young men who surrounded him and relied on him for support who caused much of the trouble. They were jealous for their idol and wanted no rival. It was they who constantly poisoned his mind against Walter. Lord Henry Howard, in particular, nursed a hatred for Walter that had no apparent cause or reason. It was to give Walter grave trouble later on. But now all was friendship between Walter and Essex, and they persuaded Robert Cecil to support the enterprise they were urging on the queen.

Cecil's dearly loved wife had died in January. Shattered by grief, he shut himself up in his London house and would see no one, though Walter wrote to him with loving sympathy. Slowly the little man pulled himself out of his sorrow. Work and power were the only things left to him. He had great influence with Elizabeth now that his father was old and sick and left much of the work of government in his hands. She had made him Secretary of State and trusted his cool judgment.

A little reluctantly she agreed to the daring plan they were pressing on her. She appointed Essex commander-in-chief for the first time but shrewdly insisted on Lord Thomas Howard being made vice-admiral and Walter rear admiral. They were men of experience whom she could trust to check the fiery impetuosity of the young earl.

Ever since Cadiz she had been in a relenting mood, and that summer when Essex went to Chatham to review the fleet, she consented to receive Walter once again. It was five years since he had entered the Presence Chamber at Whitehall. He paused a moment in the doorway, remembering that time long ago when he had first captured her love and interest.

> A beauty that can easily deceive
> Th' arrest of years and creeping age outclimb.

He had written that of her once, and now it was true. She had never had beauty, only elegance, magic, enchantment. Now her face had an ageless look, a distinction that was only of bone and line and that not even the paint and powder she sometimes used could hide from those who loved her.

She received him graciously, giving him her hand to kiss, and after she had supped, she invited him to ride with her in the cool June evening. They came back laughing and talking together like old friends. He could once more resume his duties as the Captain of her Guard, and to the rage of his enemies he went with her into the Privy Chamber as familiar as he had ever been. The years of exile were over.

Walter tried hard to remain on friendly terms with Essex, but it was not easy. The earl was thirty now but still as impetuous and irresponsible as a boy. He would agree to a plan one day and change his mind the next, exasperating Walter. Walter controlled his quick temper with difficulty, and at first everything went well between them.

In July the fleet sailed for Spain into the worst of summer storms. Buffeted by the raging seas, with sails ripped by the wind and badly leaking seams, the ships reeled back to Plymouth. The popinjay courtiers who had joyfully accompanied Essex hoping for a share of the loot and the glory found the hard uncomfortable life in a warship not at all to their liking. They were daily soaked to the skin, horribly seasick, and terrified of drowning at every violent heave of the deck.

"Thank God some of the earl's fine-weather friends have taken their gay plumes and embroidered coats back to London," remarked Arthur Gorges in Walter's cabin one day. He was sailing as captain of the *Warspite*.

His cousin looked up from the letter he was writing to Cecil. "We still have my lord of Essex with us," he said and smiled wryly. "Her Majesty will be weeping tears of joy to know her Essex is sleeping safe and sound under my hatches while his ship is being refitted."

He was fully aware that it was no longer himself but the young earl over whose safety the queen fretted as if he were her own son.

On August 17, their sails mended and their leaking timbers patched, they set out again, still dogged by atrocious weather. For ten days Walter saw neither bed nor cabin. During one night of racking wind, the mainmast snapped. He sent his squadron hurrying after Essex and galvanized the crew into repairing it in less time than seemed possible. He easily caught up with his own ships but then spent three fruitless days hunting for Essex, who had taken a different route from that planned. When Walter caught up with him off the island of Flores in the Azores, it was only to be met with sour looks and an accusation of desertion.

After a stormy scene, the earl grudgingly admitted his mistake, and it was decided that an united attack should be made on the rich island of Fayal. Walter's men were peacefully filling the water casks on shore when Essex hoisted his signal to set sail and with his usual thoughtlessness sheered off without waiting to gather his fleet. By the time Walter had picked up his sailors, the ships had vanished over the horizon, so he made all speed for Fayal, only to see nothing but an empty sea, with no sign of the earl or any of his company.

For four exasperating days his squadron idled just outside the bay, humiliated by the inhabitants, who hastily removed their goods to the hills and openly mocked the English ships that hovered so close and were too timid to attack.

Each day Walter scanned the horizon and was urged by his captains to launch an assault on the island. Soon, he thought, they would be taunting him with lack of courage, and yet he knew that Essex would deeply resent any action being taken without him.

On the fourth day he could stand it no longer. He took a small party of his sailors and led the attack himself, wading through the surf and scrambling over the steep slippery rocks despite his lame leg. They met with fierce resistance, but he marched steadily forward, putting the enemy to flight and establishing a strong point. Then Walter sent back to the ships for a small troop of land soldiers, under Essex's command though they had sailed with him. He needed them so that they could proceed, with some show of force, to the fort guarding the town.

The heat was terrific, and they advanced slowly, under constant fire, until their path was reduced to a narrow rocky gorge and to go farther without sending scouts to explore other ways into the town would have risked too many lives.

They held hasty consultation, but the soldiers hung back, not willing to venture across exposed country with so little shelter, until Walter shamed them by taking it on himself. "I will not have it said that I asked others to do what I dare not do myself," he told them.

Keymis, who would have followed him anywhere, volunteered at once, with Arthur Gorges and some of the seamen, sneering at Essex's cowardly soldiers. The bullets beat upon the old stone wall along which they were creeping. One of their company was killed; Gorges was hit in the leg, and musket shot riddled their breeches and doublet sleeves. But Walter resolutely held on. They surprised the garrison and forced the gate. Then they called up the soldiers, who shamefacedly came hurrying after them and entered the town in triumph.

The next morning the earl's ships were sighted. When Walter went aboard the flagship, he found others had been before him, only too glad to tell Essex that his rear admiral had deliberately stolen the glory that should have come to him as chief commander. Walter was received with icy coolness and immediately accused of breach of orders. Twice already Essex had altered his plans without even having the courtesy to inform him. He controlled himself with difficulty and answered quietly.

"I take myself to be a principal commander under you, my lord, and therefore not subject to martial law. When you did not come as arranged, I could only assume that you considered me strong enough to take this small island alone. My own men were accusing me of cowardice behind my back."

His dignity and restraint in face of insults had an effect on everyone, but Essex was bitterly jealous of the man whose experience and foresight were so superior to his own. He, the commander-in-chief, was being made to look a fool. He threatened Walter with a court-martial, he swore he would have him hanged out of hand, he arrested all those who had followed Walter into the attack, despite Walter's generous protest that he alone was responsible. The situation was growing worse every hour until Lord Thomas came to Walter privately, begging him to apologize even though he was in the right. "You know how it is," he said and smiled as one sensible man to another. "You have been too successful. My lord of Essex cannot endure anyone else to win the praise he thinks due only to himself."

It was some time before Walter would bend his pride, but he yielded at last, more for the sake of his officers than of himself, and an uneasy peace was patched up. Essex, however, was as exasperating as ever. Since Walter had captured Fayal, he had to conquer the island of Saint Michael. Walter obeyed his orders scrupulously, creating a diversion along the coast while Essex attacked the enemy in the rear. But the plan was never carried out. The earl and his party spent six days reveling in the captured town, leaving Walter with no information and uncertain whether to expect a victorious army or take his seamen to the rescue. The young Earl of Southampton allowed sixteen treasure ships to slip through his fingers while he and his crew ransacked one. It was maddening to realize that, without these bungling courtly amateurs, he and Lord Thomas between them might have turned costly failure into resounding success.

When they returned to England in October, they were met with alarming news. The Spanish fleet had slipped past them and was ravaging the Cornish coast. While Essex raced to London, Walter went ashore as soon as possible to calm the panic-stricken villages and take active measures for defense.

Whitehall buzzed with gossip about the quarrel between the Lord General and his rear admiral. Essex in his report had taken care to make no mention of the capture of Fayal, but Elizabeth was well aware of the truth. She was angry with Essex for his treatment of Walter, and still more angry at his mismanagement of the whole enterprise. She had tried hard to turn him into a responsible leader and statesman and he had failed her. That winter she created old Admiral Howard Earl of Nottingham, which gave him, as head of the navy, precedence over all other earls. Essex, like a spoiled child whose favorite toy has been taken away from him, immediately refused to attend either the court or the council meetings, sending the insolent excuse that they made his head ache. There were moments when Elizabeth grew very tired of her favorite's waywardness.

After three strenuous years, Walter was enjoying the peace and quiet of Sherborne. During the winter, pain flared up in his damaged leg, and exposure to all weathers in Guiana and on board ship had set up rheumatic agues. Bess urged him to go to Bath and take the cure. Reluctantly he soaked himself in the hot medicinal springs. "I am worse for the bath, not the better," he grumbled, disgustedly sipping the boiling sulfur water that tasted like bad eggs.

He had leisure now to develop his lands. His gardeners were laying out a bowling green and setting out the flowers and rare plants his sea captains brought him. He had the river diverted so that from the windows of the new house they could look out over a broad lake where swans and water birds nested. Then there was Wat. He was five years old now and had been running wild for far too long. Father and son were at last getting to know one another.

Bess came into his study one morning to find him bouncing the little boy up and down on his sound knee while they chanted together the jingly verses he had written for him:

> Three things there be, the wood, the weed, the wag—
> The wood is that which makes the gallow tree;
> The weed is that which strings the hangman's bag;
> The wag, my pretty knave, betokeneth thee.

On the last word he gave an upward jerk that shot the child into the air. Wat screamed with delight and threw his arms around his father's neck.

But it was high time for him to start lessons. Walter engaged a tutor, a gentle scholarly man called John Talbot, and at Bess's urging he asked Robert Cecil to let his motherless boy spend the summer months with them.

Will Cecil was nearly seven, a tall thin child with large hazel eyes like his father's and legs like two sticks. He was so frail that Bess longed to fatten him up and bring some healthy color into his pale little face.

The friendship between Walter and Cecil had grown more intimate. In the summer months Cecil's coach often came rumbling down the London road and turned into the park. He brought a fine Indian hawk as a gift, and Bess embroidered gloves in gold and silver thread for him. There was a new friend, too, who came visiting at Sherborne. Henry Brooke, Lord Cobham, had only just succeeded to his father's title. As the brother of Cecil's dead wife, he was one of their intimate circle. His good looks and charm of manner had won a smile from the queen, much to the jealousy of the Essex party. They saw their master offending his royal mistress by his sulks while this pushing young man was receiving the favors that might have been theirs. Cobham's openly expressed admiration for Walter endeared him to Bess and successfully concealed his lack of stability, his foolish vanity, and love of intrigue. Cecil saw him very clearly and took good care to tell him nothing, but Walter, partly to please his wife, partly because he felt at peace with all the world, fell deeper into friendship with him than he ever intended and the young man boasted of it to everyone.

It was Ireland that caused the crisis of 1598. Rebellion had broken out again under a new leader, the powerful and astute Earl of Tyrone. English settlers were attacked, their houses burned, their lands ravaged. Walter's Irish estates suffered serious damage, and Edmund Spenser was driven out of Kilcolman. The appointment of a new Lord Deputy capable of subduing the rebels became a burning problem. The queen favored one candidate and the Earl of Essex another. One morning when she rejected his proposal, he deliberately turned his back on her, his face blazing with contemptuous anger. Furious at the rebuff to her royal dignity, Elizabeth boxed his ears and bade him "get gone and be hanged!" The earl's hand flew to his sword, and if the old admiral had not intervened, there was no knowing what he might have done. He stormed out of the court in a tearing rage, swearing that he would not have taken such an insult from old King Henry VIII himself.

Walter heard the story from Robert Cecil. It was clear that something would have to be done about this young man, or else he would ruin them all. When the tragedy did come, however, it was the earl who brought it on himself.

11 : *"Sweet England's Pride Is Gone"*

—Anonymous Song

The crudely printed ballad sheet had been fastened to the gate of Durham House. It flapped in the strong March wind as Walter rode through, but he did not glance at it. He had no need. The abuse was being flung in his face wherever he went in the city:

> Essex for vengeance cries,
> His blood upon thee lies
> Mounting above the skies.
> Damnable fiend of hell,
> Mischievous Machiaevel!

Only a few weeks before, on Ash Wednesday, February 25, 1601, Robert Devereux, Earl of Essex, had been beheaded on

Tower Green, and the London mob that idolized him, that never remembered he had not so much as lifted a finger on their behalf, now wept at his death. They spat vindictively at the two men who had brought him to it, for Robert Cecil was coupled with Walter in their hatred. Only Cecil and Walter had not done so; the one person responsible for his tragic end was the queen.

The past two years, which had started with so much promise for Walter, were now ending in a mood of black gloom. Walking in Lord Burghley's funeral procession when Essex had been a pallbearer, Walter had been very much aware that with the old man's death the struggle for power between the earl, Cecil, and himself would became more open and more ugly.

In March 1599, Essex had gone to Ireland as Lord Deputy, and before he left rode past the cheering citizens, who crowded London's streets, waving banners and throwing flowers before his horse's hoofs. Will Shakespeare over at the Globe Theatre had praised him in exultant verse, comparing him to the young King Harry returning triumphant from Agincourt. Only Essex had not yet won his victories.

"Ireland, the graveyard of every general's reputation!" thought Walter as he watched the gaily dressed procession of nobles and gentlemen following after the earl. Essex was no military genius; all he longed for was the glory. His fine coat and gallant show would not carry him far in the bogs and wastelands around Dublin.

Walter glanced at Robert Cecil standing beside him and just for a second saw a flash of pure hatred in his friend's eyes. Then it was gone. He was gentle, quiet, and reserved as usual.

The months of Essex's absence from court were happy ones for Walter, despite alarming reports from Ireland and the queen's anger at the lost opportunities. "I give my lord of Essex a thousand pounds a day to go on progress!" she exclaimed angrily to her council.

One day toward the end of September the court was at the palace of Nonsuch in Surrey and Walter was in attendance as usual. It was early and the queen was still dressing. He was leaning against the doorpost of the Privy Chamber, talking idly to young Cobham, when a tall stooping figure, untidy, mud-splashed after hard riding, his whip still in his hand, pushed rudely past and made toward the door of Elizabeth's bedchamber. Walter started after him but Cobham caught him by the arm. "Let be. It is my lord of Essex."

Walter followed after to see that it was indeed Essex flinging open the bedroom door. He saw the queen, half dressed, her gray hair falling about her thin face, turn with surprise, and he saw the earl stumble to his knees, kiss her hands, put his arms around her waist. Walter would have entered, since the earl seemed half crazed, but Elizabeth made a sign to her lady-in-waiting to close the door.

It had been a strange day, but it had seen the beginning of the end. Recovered from the shock of surprise, Elizabeth had been icily angry. Essex was placed in close custody and wrote letter after letter of complaint and pleading, desperately trying to excuse his own incompetence. With a large and well-equipped army, he had frittered away every chance in romantic escapades and useless skirmishes. When at last he did move his troops against the Earl of Tyrone, he still achieved nothing, holding long parleys with the rebel leader instead of fighting with him. He had made a truce giving in to every humiliating condition and had thrown away all his advantages. Then in panic he left everything in chaos and rushed back to England to plead a futile, muddled story of injustice, accusing Ralegh, Cecil, and

Cobham of treachery and persecution. He seemed to live in a dream that had no basis in reality.

During the weeks of Essex's imprisonment, Walter saw the queen wavering between love and anger. She asked advice from everyone and took none of it. When he wrote to Robert Cecil one day, Walter had urged that Essex be banished from court and from public life. He was a danger to his queen, to his country, and to themselves. Cecil made no reply. He judged the queen quite coolly. He knew that what she feared most was an attack upon her royal authority, that she would not allow any man to overrule her judgment, however dear he had been to her, and that the final decision rested only with her.

After the tribunal that had judged Essex's actions in Ireland and forced him to admit his failure, he had been released and might in time have been forgiven, though the queen would not receive him and had cut off the grants that supplied most of his income. But, deeply in debt, he was driven to frenzy by his supporters, who thought only of their own future. Their wild talk came close to treason. Letters went between Essex and the young King of Scotland, whose eyes were fixed so greedily on the English throne. As son of Mary Queen of Scots and great-grandson of Henry VIII's sister Margaret, he was the heir who would succeed on Elizabeth's death, although she still obstinately refused to acknowledge it.

More than a year passed before the desperate and confused Essex at last forced the interview that he had been denied. He thrust himself into the queen's presence before the astonished Guard were able to prevent him. When Walter would have intervened, Elizabeth restrained him. The hand that held him back was trembling but her face was hard as stone.

"Who gave you leave, my lord, to break in here against my express command?"

Essex threw himself at her feet. "Imprison me, pronounce sentence against me, only grant me your forgiveness."

"In very truth, you have thrown back in my face every kindness I have shown to you."

Walter had withdrawn a little, but he saw Essex's face darken and heard his voice rise in anger.

"You are not only denying me my honor, but you are stealing my very means of life."

"By God's son," exclaimed Elizabeth with a scalding contempt. "What I took for abundance of heart is no more than a plea for a grant of revenue!"

Essex got to his feet, his face dangerous. The words came thickly from him. "There is no mercy in you, no kindness," he blurted out. "There is only a canker where your heart should be. Your mind is as crooked as your carcass."

He turned on his heel and with his thrusting walk pushed his way out, and on the queen's face Walter saw clearly the doom Essex had drawn down on himself. Those cruel words hurt her more deeply than his disobedience, his fumbling incompetence, and his treachery. She saw herself as he saw her, an old woman without beauty or charm. "I will break him of his will and pull down his great heart!" she cried out in anger. It was a terrible moment that Walter found hard to forget.

After that, events moved very quickly. Essex had listened more and more to his friends, the young men who were blinded by his popularity and his successful intrigues with the Scottish king. Forgetting all caution, they had persuaded the players at the Globe to revive Shakespeare's *Richard II*, with its daring scene of a king's abdication. In Essex House a conspiracy was being hatched to take the queen prisoner and put her back on the throne only on condition that Walter, Cecil, and Cobham were dismissed and Essex put at her right hand to rule the kingdom. The love between Elizabeth and her people was the deepest and strongest emotion of her life, and Essex was deliberately attacking it in trying to rouse her subjects against her. "By God's son," she exclaimed. "I am no queen. That man is above me!"

Walter did what he could to point out their folly by writing to his cousin, Ferdinando Gorges, who was one of the Essex party. The conspirators refused to let Ferdinando meet him except in a boat on the Thames in full view of Essex House. Walter kept strictly to his own side of the bargain, coming alone and unarmed. As he stood up in the rocking boat, shots spattered the water around him; he was bitterly contemptuous of men who could not even keep their word.

Ferdinando was unhappy. "Go, go, Sir Walter, if you would not lose your life," he said. "I swear we intend no harm to Her Majesty, but my lord of Essex has suffered great wrongs at her hands."

"What wrongs, in the name of God? He has had only justice," was Walter's reply. "Leave him. There is a warrant out for your arrest."

"It is too late. I have gone too far to draw back," said his cousin. "We are resolved to live or die free men."

"What can you do against the queen's authority?" asked Walter.

"It is the abuse of that authority by you and those like you," retorted Ferdinando, "that makes honest men seek for reformation of the government."

It was hopeless. Walter could not make his cousin realize the craziness of the plot in which he had become involved.

Returning to Durham House, Walter sent a message to Cecil,

but Cecil already had the situation under control. Essex came riding through the city of London at the head of his party, crying out that Ralegh and Cobham were about to murder him. "For the queen, for the queen!" he shouted. "A plot is laid for my life!" The people stared at him in amazement. They took refuge in their houses and shops. They put up their shutters. He had thought he had only to raise his hand and they would flock to his banner but now he rode through streets that were silent and deserted, and he realized the madness of what he had done. The city gates were closed against him. The heralds were already proclaiming him traitor. When he returned to Essex House, he and his supporters were arrested.

At his trial Essex was insolent, wildly abusing Walter and accusing Robert Cecil of treachery, but he broke down at his condemnation. In the Tower he gave way and made a full confession, involving everyone who had been close to him, even his own sister.

The queen was not vindictive. Only the ringleaders among the earl's supporters were condemned to death. The foolish young Earl of Southampton was sent to the Tower, and Walter successfully pleaded for his cousin's life.

On a cold morning when frost crisped the grass and furred the leafless branches of the trees, a sad procession moved toward Tower Green. As Captain of the Guard, Walter was obliged to be present, but the watching crowd, their eyes fixed on Essex, murmured against him and he withdrew to the White Tower to watch from the windows of the armory. Long afterward, in answer to the slanders that had been spoken about him, he was to say: "God I take to witness, my eyes shed tears for him when he died and as I hope to look in the face of God hereafter, my lord of Essex did not see my face when he suffered."

After that bleak and distressing scene, Walter returned to Durham House. In the streets, they were singing a new ballad to a sad and haunting melody:

> Sweet England's pride is gone!
>   welladay! welladay!
> Brave honour graced him still,
>   gallantly, gallantly;
> He ne'er did deed of ill,
>   well it is known;
> But Envy, that foul fiend
>   whose malice ne'er did end,
> Hath brought true virtue's friend
>   Unto his thrall.

In his study high up in the turret Walter stared out over the gray water. Sometimes it seemed to him that all his ambition, all his striving after wealth and fame were worth nothing. You watch another man's tragedy, he thought, you know too well the promise and the threat, but there is a bright glory in the world that is too tempting and you cannot prevent yourself reaching out after it. When he watched Essex die that morning, he had had the strangest feeling that he too had seen the best of his days.

12 : *"Leave Every Man Free"*

—Walter Ralegh

Young Wat was having his portrait painted. He was nine years old, and he felt very important standing beside his father wearing his best doublet and breeches of striped green velvet, his face scrubbed, his hair well brushed, and a new sword slung from his belt just as if he were grown up. Master Marc Gheerhaerts, the painter, with a face round and red as one of his native Dutch cheeses, had hung a deep orange curtain behind them, and he frowned severely if Wat so much as wrinkled his nose when a fly crawled across it. It was hard to keep still with pins and needles shooting up one leg and Will Cecil making faces at him from behind the artist's back, but he stood very upright, his left hand on his hip, looking straight before him. He wanted to look just like his father, who was magnificent in deep-yellow damask richly embroidered in gold. All the same,

National Portrait Gallery

Sir Walter and his son Wat

Wat was glad when he was released and he could go racing off with Will, who still spent more time with them than with his father.

Last year, when the queen had appointed Walter governor of Jersey in the Channel Islands, Bess had taken the two children to see him go on board the *Antelope* at Weymouth. Afterward they had gone sea-bathing, jumping up and down in the waves, to the astonishment of those staring at them from the beach. Fancy plunging into ice-cold salt water for the sake of the children's health, they murmured, shaking their heads doubtfully at one another. No one dreamed of doing such a dangerous thing. It was just the kind of extraordinary notion that Sir Walter would think up!

To the disappointment of the two boys, Walter returned from Jersey only to go immediately to London for the opening of Parliament. He was not quite like other fathers. Though he kept a strict watch over their lessons, he was also the leader in all their games. Wat knew all about his ships. Sometimes when the *Mary Spark* or the *Roebuck* went off to Guiana as one or another did every year, Walter would take his son with him to Plymouth. He would answer the boy's eager questions, promising that one day, when he was a little older, they would go together and he would see for himself the fabulous land his father had so often described. Will was more timid. He was afraid of the sea, but he was as enthusiastic as Wat when they sailed their toy ships on the lake in mock battles against the Spaniards. Walter was teaching them both to handle a sword, and sometimes he would ride with them across the heath and let them fly their small hawks alongside his great Indian peregrine. This year he was away in London so long that Will made up his mind to write a letter and ask Lady Ralegh to send it when the courier took the usual weekly packet.

"Dear Sir Walter," he began, nibbling the end of the long quill pen and trying hard not to make too many blots. "We must all exclaim and cry out because you will not come down. You being absent, we are like soldiers that when their captain is absent, they do not know what to do. You are so busy about idle matters. Sir Walter, I will be plain with you. I pray leave all idle matters and come down to us."

Walter smiled a little sadly when he read it. The child's warm affection cheered him when daily he was opposing Robert Cecil in Parliament and a distinct coolness had come between them. They sat side by side on the same bench, and when they rose to speak, they were often arguing against one another. More and more often, Walter was finding himself on the side of the poor and even the beggars. Many of them, he would argue, were discharged soldiers and seamen, penniless and disabled through serving their country. He scornfully criticized the meanness of the rich, who called it good policy to squeeze the pockets of the poor and oppress their liberties. Just as he had fought for his tin miners, he opposed Cecil's attempt to regulate the private life of the citizens by laws that would give them coarser bread and thinner beer and would even force farmers to change from sheep-grazing to the growing of corn. He had grown up on his father's farm. He knew how impossible it was for poor countrymen to find the gold for expensive seed. "Let every man be free to use his fields for that for which they are most fitted," he said. "Leave every man free, which is the desire of a true Englishman."

His clear-cut arguments defeated the bill, but he could not help but notice how Cecil resented the way the members of the Commons followed his advice. Money was needed urgently both for the war in Ireland and for defense against renewed

Spanish aggression. Taxes were the only answer, but they hit hard at the poor with their tiny incomes.

Cecil spoke in a fine burst of patriotic fervor. "Neither pot nor pan, nor dish nor spoon, should be spared when danger is at our elbow. Let the King of Spain know we are willing to sell our all in defense of God's religion, our prince, and our country."

There were villagers so destitute they owned only one cooking pot, one dish, and a single spoon. Some of the wives of Walter's sailors had even less. Sarcastically he replied, "I do not care that our enemies should know we are selling pots and pans to pay taxes. My honorable friend calls it policy; does it not rather argue poverty in our state?"

Francis Bacon, that subtle and clever lawyer who had once been Essex's friend, insisted that the poor should be taxed as heavily as the rich, since it was only right that everyone should pull together in equal yoke.

Confounded hypocrite, thought Walter as, stung by his smug complacency, he rose to his feet. "Call you it an equal yoke if a poor man pays as much as a rich man when his estate may be no better than he is assessed and ours are entered in the queen's book at not the hundredth part of their wealth?"

He had shocked them all, this time. His outrageous frankness about his own class and their privileges disturbed the members more than anything else. Before they knew what he was about, he would have them paying all the taxes and leaving the peasants free! Where justice and freedom were concerned, he was always too outspoken. Carried away by his own passionate fervor, he did not realize how much he had offended them all, Robert Cecil among them.

He took Cecil's arm as they went down the steps together,

urging him to come down to Sherborne and smiling as he pulled out Will's letter to show him.

Cecil thought of the stiff formal notes in careful Latin sent to him by his son and felt his heart shrink with a bitter envy. Walter had won his boy's love as easily as that of his own son. Will must come home. When Walter protested that it was a pity to take the child away when he was so happy with them and so much improved in health, Cecil was even more determined to do so.

Cecil was disturbed by other matters more important to him than his son's affection. Ever since Essex's death, the queen had been showing more and more favor to Walter. Had he got rid of the earl only to put a more capable and dangerous rival in his place? Jersey had never been so well governed as it was under Walter's rule. Cecil had successfully prevented him from being appointed to the Privy Council, but he was always being called upon unofficially for his advice. When distinguished foreign visitors came to England, it was always Walter who greeted and entertained them. "I arrest you as my prisoner in the queen's name," he said jestingly to the superb Duc de Sully, the celebrated minister of Henri IV of France, when he arrived incognito in London.

"I should consider such an imprisonment the greatest honor," replied the duc, charmed by the Englishman who looked so magnificent and spoke such fluent French.

With all his knowledge of men and the world, Walter still believed in friendship and loyalty. He still found it painful when those he trusted betrayed and cheated him. Sometimes it struck him that Cecil was not as warm in friendship as he had been, though he still visited them at Sherborne and invested money in the profitable trading ventures. But Walter's life was far too busy. His official duties, the improvement of Sherborne, his intellectual circle, which had widened to include poets and writers seeking his patronage, filled his days to overflowing. Occasionally when he was in the mood, he would sup at the Mermaid Tavern in Cheapside, where he would meet Ben Jonson, with the actors from the Globe, the playwrights and journalists, all the wits of the town, holding them entranced with the brilliance of his conversation. His long carved pipe rested on his knee, the thick smoke curling up into the dark beard. His embroidered satin doublet with its jeweled buttons and the priceless white lace at throat and wrists brought a glimpse of the great world of the court into their impoverished lives.

Parliament had moved into the stormiest session Walter had ever known. The members of the House of Commons were feeling their strength. They were attacking the queen herself, challenging her constitutional power. Elizabeth, with her shrewd political insight, knew that they were gaining force, that the voice of the people would one day be heard more and more and that the time would soon come when the members would put their principles before loyalty to their sovereign. But it would not be her battle, though she must make the first concession. She called a deputation to her, giving gracious assent to their demands, promising that certain taxes would be remitted and others closely examined.

"I thank God that he has made me a queen over so thankful a people," she said to them, "yet this I count the glory of my crown, that I have reigned with your loves."

Those words of hers brought them kneeling at her feet, rapturously kissing her hands.

"Though you have had and may have many mightier and

The New York Public Library Picture Collection

Sir Walter (*third from right*) enjoying the company of Shakespeare
(*seated center*) and Ben Jonson (*leaning on table*) among others

wiser princes sitting in this seat," she went on, "yet you never had, nor shall have, any to love you better."

Old and tired though she was—that very morning she had nearly fainted as she waited to receive the deputation—her heart was still as brave as a lion, thought Walter. She won them to her as she had done long ago at the time of the Armada, and his own heart was as warm with affection for her now as it had been then.

But after that splendid surge of loyalty, a reaction set in. Young men who had not been born when the crown was placed on her head were discontented and looked for change. They had been ruled by a woman long enough. A king was a new word, a new spur to ambition, and they waited impatiently for the time to come when James would reign in her place.

One day in the summer of 1602 Cecil brought Lord Henry Howard to Elizabeth and she disliked him at once. There was something chilling about his pale, thin mouth and hooded eyes as cold and venomous as a snake's. She glanced from him to the little man she called her "Pygmy" and felt suddenly depressed. Where were the brilliant men who had once graced her court? All dead, all gone—Leicester with his gypsy beauty, austere clever Walsingham, dear Burghley who had been guide and councilor, and Essex, that handsome headstrong boy for whom she still mourned. Of them all, only Walter remained, and at this moment he was far away in Jersey and this small, mean man was gnawing away at him like a rat, trying to persuade her, the queen, who had proved his loyalty through more than twenty years, that he was plotting against her. She was not for a moment deceived. She just felt tired of them, tired of the whole weary business of being a queen. She dismissed them curtly.

National Portrait Gallery

William Cecil, 1st Baron Burghley

Cecil and his new friend walked away together after the interview. Lord Howard was small and insignificant, with no charm of face or grace of manner. He was a Catholic, brother to the Duke of Norfolk whom Elizabeth had beheaded and son to the Earl of Surrey whom her father had sent to the block. All his life he had been on the edge of treasonable plots. He hated all Tudors and bore a grudge against the men Elizabeth favored. He had only just avoided disaster in Essex's ruin, and in Cecil had found an unexpected ally. For years he had longed to destroy Walter and now he saw his opportunity. Although the queen would not listen to him, she could not live much longer, and when the Scottish king came to the throne, it would be different.

Sitting beside Lord Henry in the coach that carried them away from the palace, Cecil remembered what his father had once said to him. "No wise man continues in a friendship that might deprive him of his own ambitions." He knew only too well that despite all his hard work and high office as Secretary of State, he had no personal charm, no popularity, no power to draw men to him.

> Backed like a lute case,
> Bellied like a drum,
> Like Jackanapes on horseback
> Sits little Robin Thumb.

As much as he tried to ignore them, the cruel ballads written about him ran through his mind. He couldn't help but wonder what sort of an impression he would make on the young King of Scots, who was known for his unstable temperament and strange likes and dislikes. He thought that Walter, with his brilliant mind, his magnetic personality, the charm that had won Elizabeth's friendship, could easily sway the new king to the unconventional free-thinking that he so distrusted. He must make sure that would not happen by destroying Walter's reputation in the king's eyes before ever he met him. Walter made it fatally easy for him to do so. He was the only one among the great men at court who did not rush to curry favor with the King of Scotland. When James's envoy, the Earl of Lennox, had visited London, going secretly from one courtier to another with promises of future favors in return for their support, Walter's refusal to have anything to do with it was courteous but firm. He was too deeply obliged to the mistress he had served so long to seek favor elsewhere, he said, and he could not now diminish his respect for his own sovereign.

So Cecil and Lord Howard sent letters to Scotland filled with slanders against Walter, who, quite unaware of his friend's treachery, was spending his time reorganizing the economy of Jersey and strengthening its defenses. One day, while he waited for a fair wind to carry his ship back to England, he listened idly to Lord Cobham, who had come over in the *Antelope* to visit him. Cobham had become involved in some preposterous intrigue with Count d'Aremberg, the Spanish minister in Holland, and was trying hard to interest Walter in it.

"If you could bring yourself to work for a peace," he was saying, "Spain would pay you fifty thousand crowns without a question being asked."

The very idea that he who had fought the Spaniards all his life should now ally himself with them was so ridiculous that he did not even feel it necessary to be serious. "I should need far more than that," he answered carelessly.

"When Elizabeth dies, there are others with just as good a claim to the throne as the Scottish king," Cobham went on eagerly. "There is Arabella Stuart, for instance. She is the great-granddaughter of Henry VIII's sister just as James is the great-grandson, and she is a woman. Put her on the throne and you would be in a position to rule the kingdom."

"My dear Henry," said Walter, "I met her once when I dined with the Lord Admiral. She is an empty-headed little ninny without a thought beyond her suitors and her fine gowns. No one in their senses would ever choose her as queen."

He changed the subject, discussing the new defenses he had built around the island and sketching idly the strategy an enemy would have to employ for a successful invasion. He wondered if he ought to warn Robert Cecil of his brother-in-law's treasonable talk, except that it seemed too absurd to come to anything and he did not want to get the young man into more trouble with Robert than he was already.

But once Walter was back in England, Cobham was in and out of Durham House every day, always busy with some new intrigue, until Walter was weary of it. He had begun to realize how foolish he had been to encourage so much intimacy between them, but he found it difficult to turn a cold shoulder on someone he had once called friend.

It was in the spring of 1603, when he was busy with military defenses at Plymouth, that he received the terrible news. He stood on the castle rampart looking out over the sea and tried to believe it. Elizabeth had died on March 24 at three o'clock in the morning after a short illness, and the last gesture she had made, when she was already unable to speak, was to acknowledge James VI of Scotland as her heir. Walter had not seen her since the Christmas revels, when she had danced one night in a gold dress thin and light as a candle flame so that it had been difficult to realize that time was catching up with her.

Now she was gone, the woman whom he had loved and

served with such devotion, but there was no time for grief. He must think of his future and that of his wife and son. He started for London immediately. Everyone of note had already ridden northward to meet James on his slow triumphant journey from Scotland. With a reluctance he could not explain to himself, Walter turned his horse's head toward Huntingdon. It was high time he too kissed the new king's hand.

13 : *"My Death was Determined"*

—Walter Ralegh

James VI of Scotland and I of England was thirty-seven. He had light brown hair, blue eyes, and a rosy complexion, but there the resemblance to his beautiful mother abruptly stopped. His figure was already running to fat, he dressed badly and walked ungracefully. Crowned king when still only a baby of thirteen months, he had been brought up by stern tutors without love or kindness and was bullied by ambitious Scottish nobles who had conspired against him and twice threatened to murder him. He still lived in constant fear of assassination. Thankfully he left his backward, poverty-stricken country behind him and looked forward to the rich, civilized society of his new kingdom.

The English courtiers hurrying to welcome him hid their dismay at first sight of their new sovereign. There was no doubt about it, one of them wrote, he slobbered when he spoke, "his tongue being too large for his mouth, which made him drink very uncomely as if eating his drink, which came out into the cup each side of his mouth. His skin was soft as taffeta sarsenet, which felt so because he never washed his hands, only rubbed his finger ends slightly with the wet end of a napkin. . . . His clothes were made large and easy, the doublets quilted for stiletto proof, his breeches in great pleats and full stuffed, and he would never change his garments until worn out to the very rags."

One of his Scottish courtiers had once remarked that if he were shut away for seven years and then released, he could tell where the king had been every day during that time and what dishes he had eaten, from the state of his doublet.

He had been well educated and could be witty and intelligent, but he was also heartily jealous of anyone showing more learning than himself. Some of his Scots made deliberate mistakes in their Latin to give their master the pleasure of correcting them. He had a crude sense of humor and shocked everyone by ordering a thief to be hanged out of hand on his journey south. It was pointed out respectfully that such barbarous customs were not usual in England, where every citizen, no matter how mean, was given a fair trial before he was executed. "If the new king hangs a man before he is tried," said Sir John Harington jestingly, "will he then try a man before he has offended?"

This was the man then whom Walter saw when Cecil presented him and he went down on his knees.

"Ralegh! Ralegh!" mumbled James in his thick Scottish accent. "And rawly have we heard o' ye, mon!"

Walter ignored the petty punning jibe as he kissed the unkingly hand extended to him, still quite unaware of the poison poured into James's ears by his enemies. Treason, atheism, witchcraft, had all been alleged against him. He is "the greatest Lucifer that hath lived in our age," Henry Howard had written. "Hell did never vomit up such a couple" as he and Lord Cobham. "A man most religious men do hold anathema," added Cecil. "In pride he exceeds all men alive and he will stop at nothing to gain his own ends. He carries himself with such an awe and ascendancy over other mortals."

Walter, accustomed to Elizabeth's fastidious taste, had taken the trouble to wash off the mud stains of travel and dress fittingly for the royal reception. Tall, spare and elegant, his thick curling hair only lightly touched with gray, still graceful despite his limp, he made James painfully aware of his own awkward figure and shambling walk, his scanty beard and food-stained doublet. And then Walter made two mistakes. He referred to the late queen in unmistakable tones of grief when James had expressly commanded that no mention of her death should be made in his presence, and when the king made a half-jesting remark that he might have had to fight for his kingdom, Walter burst out with "Would to God you had! Then Your Majesty would have known your friends from your foes!"

He could scarcely have said anything more disturbing to a man who had lived all his life in fear and who shook with terror at the sight of an unsheathed sword.

Walter realized that he was unwelcome and could think of no reason for it. No doubt this awkward, shabby young Scot would soon learn better manners at the English court. He shrugged off the coolness as something that would presently right itself and two days later was riding back to London for the queen's funeral.

The long procession wound its impressive way through the hushed streets, the only sounds the muffled beat of the drum,

"My Death was Determined" : 153

the slow tolling of the bells, and the sobs of the people crowding the sidewalks. The Guards brought up the rear, walking with their halberds reversed. Walter was at their head in his silver armor, black plumes in his helmet, a scarf of mourning on his arm, and desolation in his heart.

He thought back to those first years when he had been so high in her favor, two keen minds taking fire from one another, turning every moment into joy. He had felt unconquerable but for her affection for Essex and her cruelty during the five long years after his marriage. After their reconciliation they had been good friends, had shared the same interests, had argued and laughed together. "The blossom's fallen, the sap's gone from the tree," he had written once. It was only too true now.

The open chariot was drawn by four horses caparisoned in black velvet embroidered with the arms of England and France. It carried the magnificent casket beneath a gold-encrusted pall, the waxen effigy of Elizabeth in the robes of state bobbing above it like a horrible mockery of her life that had been filled with such energy. Now he had to brace himself to face a new age and serve a king whom already he doubted if he could respect. As he watched the coffin being lowered into the vault in Westminster Abbey, he felt as if part of himself was buried with the queen he had so loved.

All too quickly Walter's fortunes began to fall. In May he was curtly informed that one of James's Scottish courtiers would replace him as Captain of the Guard. In an attempt to save his position, Walter only made matters worse. He presented the king with a good sound plan for a new attack against Spain, offering to raise two thousand men at his own expense. It was excellent in every respect, except that James wanted no war. Peace at any price was what he desired. He hated the very idea of conflict and from childhood had had an obsession about weapons of any kind. How powerful this man must be, he thought, who talked so confidently of leading an army into battle. If he could raise two thousand men for his king, he could raise as many against him. He must be taught a sharp lesson.

In June Walter was ordered to leave Durham House, his home for twenty years. He had spent a fortune on it, and it was handsomely furnished and provisioned for months ahead. He protested indignantly that a fortnight to move his household in was less than the time granted to the humblest villager in the meanest cottage. But this was still not the worst. Steps were being taken to strip his other posts from him.

"He must move against the king now," muttered Henry Howard, rubbing his thin dry hands with pleasure. "He is still powerful in the West. France or Spain would leap at the offer of his sword. His pride will never let him accept such humiliation." But Cecil knew better. Raleghs had been loyal for over four hundred years. It was they who would have to take the first step, and the ill luck that was dogging Walter gave them their opportunity.

There had recently been discovered a Catholic conspiracy to capture the king and his family, to hold them prisoner until he agreed to freedom for their religion, and if necessary destroy him and the royal children. Deeply involved in the plot was Lord Cobham's younger brother, George Brooke. He was unstable and irresponsible, and when he was arrested, he implicated all his closest friends, including his older brother. Cobham, confronted with an accusation of treason, remembered all those talks with Walter in Jersey and at Durham House, all those times when Walter had half listened and laughed and made no particular protest. Out of terror, he put the blame squarely on his friend.

On a day in July Walter was pacing up and down the terrace at Windsor. The king had reached the South, but plague was raging in London and he was afraid to enter the city. Here in the great forests surrounding Windsor Castle the king could indulge in his favorite sport of hunting. As usual, the Privy Council had accompanied the king, and when their morning council meeting was over, they would all be riding out with him to hunt the deer. Walter was leaning on the parapet when Cecil came out and took his arm. "Come in for a moment," he said. "The council wishes to ask you a few questions."

Coming from the sunshine into the shaded room, he looked hard at the men grouped around the long table. They asked him immediately what he knew of Lord Cobham's dealings with the Spanish minister in the Netherlands. He had to think very quickly, and he cursed himself for having been so unguarded in the past. Had he ever expressed open disloyalty to the king? Cobham had talked some nonsense about Spain offering him a bribe for his support and he had said jestingly that he would need a great deal of money to betray his country and ally himself with the enemy. Surely no one could take seriously a casual conversation over a supper table. He answered cautiously, and finally was told that he would be kept in custody for the time being.

Cobham was interrogated once more and tied himself in knots of lies. "It is useless to persist in denial when the proof is in our hands," Cecil told him. "Sir Walter has told us the whole wretched story." Cecil then read a few carefully chosen sentences from a letter Walter had written to him after his questioning and, as he had hoped, Cobham leaped at once to the conclusion that Walter had betrayed his folly. He burst into the wildest accusations, trying to excuse himself. It was not he but Walter who had been responsible for the whole plot—Walter who was willing to join the enterprise if only the bribes were large enough. It was Walter who had pursued him with it day and night and would never let the matter rest.

Back in his cell after the merciless grilling, Cobham regained his balance and took back every word, as frantic in denial as he had been in accusation, but the council now had something in writing, and Walter was put in the Tower.

The first few weeks of his imprisonment nearly drove Walter out of his mind. That he should be accused of conspiring with Spain was so unbelievable that he would not accept it. It must be a mistake. Only very slowly did he come to realize that with Elizabeth's death not only had he lost the royal favor but he was exposed to vicious attacks of enemies who had long waited for this very moment. And not only enemies—the shock of Robert Cecil's betrayal was most painful of all.

> Tell men of high condition
>   that manage the estate,
> Their purpose is ambition
>   their practice only hate.

Although he had written those words once, he had never realized their bitter truth till now. Only a few days before his arrest, Walter had written Bess at Sherborne telling her that Cecil was still his partner in one of his trading ventures and still their staunch friend. In a mood of black despair he thought of suicide. At least if he died with the case against him still unproved, his wife and son would be left untouched in their own home. But he had no weapon except a poor table knife and his tremendous vitality rose up so strongly at the thought of taking his own life that his hand shook and the miserable blade missed its mark.

If only he could have been brought face to face with Cobham, he could have demolished his accusations in an instant. But though the young man was imprisoned nearby, they were not allowed to meet and would have had no communication with one another at all if it had not been for the son of Sir George Harvey, the lieutenant governor of the Tower. Like so many youngsters, he had an intense admiration for the distinguished prisoner and he discovered that his father was deliberately holding back from the council a letter from Cobham in which he absolved Walter from all guilt. Harvey's son volunteered to act as messenger between the two prisoners. To the boy it was an exciting game. Free to go where he liked, he threw an apple through Cobham's high window with a note from Walter attached to it and received a reply by the same method. The lad was found out and clapped in prison by his angry father, but he refused to say a word and the letter was already safely tucked away in Walter's pocket until it should be needed.

The weeks dragged slowly by. It was October already, and outside his prison the leaves were piling up in great drifts, but the council were still working hard to substantiate the charges against him, although they found it a heartbreakingly difficult task. Cobham said one thing one day and denied it the next, and obstinately refused to sign his first accusation.

The others concerned in the Catholic plot refused to budge from their original statement that they loathed Walter Ralegh and would never have had anything to do with a scheme in which he was involved. It was very aggravating, but Cecil and

Henry Howard persevered all that long hot summer while the plague ravaged London. Those who could fled out of the stricken city; those who could not swallowed antidotes concocted from rosemary and rue steeped in wine and ginger. They dipped their money and even their letters into boiling vinegar to ward off infection. They prayed night and morning and fumigated their houses with burning feathers and swinging braziers of hot coals sprinkled with sweet herbs and sulfur, ambergris and juniper. Bonfires burned at street corners. Every dog and cat had been killed, but the unsuspected rats fattened and multiplied, spreading the plague wherever they went. More and more houses were chalked with the dreaded red cross and the fearful words "God have mercy on us," while at night the death carts lumbered along the streets.

The king had already hurried into the country with all his household, and it was decided that the trial should be held not at Westminster but at Winchester, sixty miles away in Hampshire. On November 10 Walter set out from the Tower in his own coach with a mounted military escort. It was a terrible journey. The London streets were packed with crowds who had braved even the plague to hurl abuse and filth at Walter. They hadn't forgotten Essex's death and they still blamed him for it. The ballad-sellers were doing a roaring trade with their farthing scandal sheets.

> Ralegh doth time bestride
> He sits 'twixt wind and tide
> Yet uphill he cannot ride
> For all his bloody pride.

"It was hob or nob," wrote Sir William Waad, who sat trembling beside him in the coach, "if Ralegh would escape alive through such multitudes of unruly people as did exclaim against him. If one hare-brained fellow had begun to set upon him as they were near to do it, no entreaty or means would have prevailed: the fury and tumult of the people were so great."

Walter was contemptuous. "Dogs do always bark at those they know not," was his only comment as he glanced at his white-faced companion. His thoughts were more painful. He knew every step of the journey. It was the road he had ridden so often to Sherborne, his beloved home with its flower gardens, its bowling green, the hawks, the hunting dogs, and the bird-haunted lake. He wondered if he would ever see any of it again.

Winchester was crammed with the judges and their retinues, the attorney general with the officers of the law, with nobles, courtiers, and hangers-on, all eager to be present at so famous a trial. A small group of Walter's humble seamen, who had tramped all the way from Devon to give him their support, raised a thin cheer as his coach lumbered up the steep hill. Wolvesey Castle was ancient, its hall long and lofty. Arthur's hall it was called, from the round table hung on the wall inscribed with the names of his long-dead knights.

The city was shrouded in a thick November fog. Walter's cell under the great hall was icy cold, the stone walls running with damp. He shivered when they clanged the door shut. Seven of the conspirators had already been tried and condemned to death. In two days he would face his accusers and learn his own fate.

Walter was roused at dawn on November 17 by the strange beastlike cry of the great horn that was still sounded at Winchester as it had been in past centuries to call men to arms. As always, he was magnificent in the face of a crisis. No one would have guessed when he entered the judgment hall that for the last two days he had been lying sick and shaking with fever on the hard prison bed.

He ran his eye over the packed courtroom. Not a seat was empty, and the public benches were crammed with an excited, chattering crowd. Eagerly they craned their necks to catch a glimpse of the prisoner. His elegance, his air of nonchalant ease astonished them. This was going to be a show worth watching. They rose to their feet as the solemn procession, gorgeous in scarlet and gold, made its entry. The three judges, the councilors, and the commissioners took their seats. The attorney general, Sir Edward Coke, his chestnut hair and beard glossy and well trimmed, took up his position. He was England's most brilliant advocate, famous not only for his mastery of the law but for his brutal cross-questioning that he was confident could reduce any man to humility.

The long duel began. The law allowed the accused no defense counsel, no calling of witnesses. Walter could rely on nothing but the keenness of his intellect and the swiftness with which he could grasp a point and answer it. He was cool and steady as the list of charges rolled ominously forth: that he and Cobham had conspired to put Arabella Stuart on the throne and destroy the king, that they had been ready to accept gold from Spain with which to raise rebellion and bring in foreign troops. To all of them he replied calmly, "Not guilty."

The first clash came early. Coke swung around on him, his head thrust forward in attack. "To whom, Sir Walter, do you bear malice? To the royal children? I will prove you the most notorious traitor that ever came to the bar."

"Prove but one of these things wherewith you have charged me and I will confess the whole indictment and that I am the most horrible traitor that ever lived, and worthy to be crucified with a thousand torments."

Sir Edward Coke,
Lord Chief Justice

Robert Cecil, 1st Earl of Salisbury.
Painting by J. De Britz (1602)

The case against him was a thin one, but Coke had marshaled it magnificently. His attacks came one after the other, sharp and stabbing; all the careless remarks that Walter had thought nothing of were being flung in his face as proofs of guilt. Bitterly he realized his folly, but he did not lose his head. He countered Coke's bullying with calm reason and presently his coolness began to rile the lawyer's fiery temper. Coke burst into more violent abuse, using the familiar and insulting "thou" as he would to a servant.

"Thou art a monster. Thou hast an English face but a Spanish heart. Now, my lords, you shall see the most horrible practices that ever came out of the bottomless pit of the lowest hell. All that Cobham did was by thy instigation, thou viper. I will prove thee the rankest traitor in all England."

"No, Master Attorney, I am no traitor. Whether I live or die, I shall stand as true a subject as ever the king hath. You may call me traitor at your pleasure, but I take comfort in it. It is all that you can do; for I do not yet hear that you charge me with any treason."

"Have I angered you?" burst out Coke eagerly.

"I am in no case to be angry."

The dignity of his reply had great effect. A little sigh of pleasure ran all around the spectators. They were not against Coke being brought down a peg or two. They settled back in their seats, prepared to enjoy themselves.

The clerk of the court read Cobham's confession, a tangled tale of truth and lies. "And this is all the evidence that can be brought against me! Poor shifts!" Walter said scornfully. But muddled and flimsy as it was, he must answer it.

He looked toward the twelve solemn men whose eyes never left his face. "Gentlemen of the jury, I pray you to understand this. This is that which must either condemn me or give me life, which must free me or send my wife and child to beg their bread about the streets. This is that which must prove me a notorious traitor or a true subject of the king." He had not been permitted pen or paper to make notes. He pulled himself together and began.

"It is true I suspected that Lord Cobham had communication with the Spanish minister, but I knew that long since in the late queen's time, as did also my lord Cecil." With dignity and quiet reason he demolished their accusations one by one, showing how baseless they were, how wildly improbable. Why, for instance, if he had wanted to plot with Spain, would he have been such a fool as to choose the present time?

"I was not so bare of sense but I saw that, if ever this state was strong, it was now that we have the kingdom of Scotland united and instead of a Lady whom Time had surprised we had now an active king. For me at this time to make myself a Robin Hood, a Wat Tyler, a Kett, or a Jack Cade! I was not so mad."

His reference to his dear dead mistress brought tears to the eyes of some of the listeners. They listened more intently as he went on.

"The state of Spain was not unknown to me. I knew his weakness, his poorness, his humbleness at this time. I knew that six times we have repulsed his forces. Thrice I served against him myself at sea, wherein for my country's sake I had expended of my own property forty thousand marks. I knew where beforetime he was wont to have forty great sail at the least in his ports, now he hath not past six or seven. I knew the King of Spain to be the proudest prince in Christendom, but now he cometh creeping to the king my master for peace."

The hall was hushed into silence. For a brief moment he had reminded them of the great days of the Armada and Cadiz. The tinge of Devon in his voice brought a breath of honesty, of the open air. This was the sailor speaking, the man of action, not the courtier. There was a long pause when the quiet voice fell silent. The audience had been impressed by his courage, the steadfast integrity that met Coke's insults with reason and calm pride. It was as if the ordinary people were seeing the real man for the first time and not the proud, disdainful, arrogant image that for so long had been the object of their hatred.

All that long and weary day he fought so gallantly for his life that one of the spectators was afterward to write: "Sir Walter answered with that temper, wit, learning, courage, and judgment that, save it went with the hazard of his life, it was the happiest day he ever spent."

Passionately he pleaded that Cobham should be brought into the court. "My lords, I claim to have my accuser brought here to speak face to face. Though I know not how to make my best defense by law, yet since I was a prisoner I have learned that by the law and statutes of this realm in case of treason a man ought to be convicted by the testimony of two witnesses. Is it so unreasonable in me to desire only one? If I have done these things, I deserve not to live, but I beseech you to let Cobham be sent for. Let him be charged upon his soul, upon his allegiance to the king, and if he will then maintain his accusation to my face, I will confess myself guilty."

But this his judges dared not do. They had suffered enough from the unstable Cobham. Brought before their prisoner, he would certainly break down and deny everything.

The Lord Chief Justice said testily, "The statute you mention, Sir Walter, does not help you. All is now judged by Common Law, and by that the accusation of a confederate in treason is proof enough."

It stung him to indignation. "If it were some small matter of an estate, you would bring a dozen witnesses, and I am being tried for my life."

The short winter day was already drawing in. The yellow fog outside shadowed the hall into an early darkness. While the candles were being lit, the judges pulled their furred robes more closely around them and the public shuffled their chilly feet into the rushes on the stone floor.

Coke was now bringing a single witness, a poor sailor who, twisting his cap in nervous fingers, repeated some gossip heard in foreign taverns and alehouses. In the port of Lisbon he had heard someone say that the King of England would never be crowned, "for his throat will be cut by Don Ralegh and Don Cobham."

Men like this could be bought for two a penny and impressed nobody. "What infer you upon that?" asked Walter contemptuously.

"That your treason hath wings," retorted Coke.

Walter gathered himself together for one last appeal. "Gentlemen of the jury, remember what St. Augustine says: So judge as if you were about to be judged yourselves. If you yourselves would like to be hazarded in your lives—your lands confiscated, your wives and children and servants left crying to the world, and all without the open testimony of a single witness—then so judge me as you yourselves would be judged."

It was a simple human appeal, rising above the words of lawyers, calling only upon the law of God. It deeply moved the ordinary people and it roused Coke to fury.

"You profess honesty and are yourself no more than a spider of hell. I want words to express your vile treasons."

"I think you want words indeed, for you have spoken the same thing half a dozen times."

Laughter ran all around the court, and Coke, beside himself, shook his fist in his face. "Damnable atheist, thou art the most vile and execrable traitor that ever lived," he shouted. "Thy name is hateful to all the realm of England for thy pride. There never lived a viler viper on the face of the earth than thou. Let all that have heard you this day judge what you are and what a traitor's heart you bear, whatever you pretend."

In his hand he held a paper, a surprise he had kept to the last, the final damning word forced only the day before from Cobham in his cell. It accused Walter of bargaining with Spain for a flat yearly pension in return for spying and passing on information as to "what was intended by England against Spain, the Low Countries, and the Indies."

It was the ridiculous offer that he had idly discussed and regarded so lightly as another of Cobham's flights of fancy. Elizabeth would never have believed such things about him. Time and time again he had listened to men talking treason and had brought the information to her. He had a sudden aching longing for the beringed hand rapping his cheek, her sharp dry voice saying, "Come, Walter, what plot have you discovered for me now?" For the first time in that endless day Walter had no ready answer, but he was still not beaten. He pulled out the letter from his pocket, the one which young Harvey had obtained for him in the Tower.

"Hear now, I pray you," he said, "what Cobham hath written to me." When Coke would have stopped him, he raised his voice. "Surely it was not ill in me to ask him to speak the truth."

It was Cecil who took the letter, putting aside Coke's outstretched hand and reading it aloud. "To clear my conscience, satisfy the world, and free myself from the cry of your blood, I protest upon my soul and before God and his Angels, I never had conference with you in any treason; nor was ever moved by you to the things I before accused you of, and for anything I know, you are as innocent and as clear from any treason against the king as is any subject living."

The jury was plainly startled. His dismayed judges argued hotly about its honesty, but they were not prepared to accept it. It had been obtained by cunning and underhand methods, urged one of them, whereas Cobham's first accusation was obtained without promise of mercy or pardon. What was not stated was that he had been bullied into signing it the night before.

The jury retired for only a bare quarter of an hour before they returned and gave their verdict of guilty.

The Lord Chief Justice began to speak. "I thought I should never see this day, to have stood in this place to give sentence of death against you, because I thought it impossible that one of so great parts should have fallen so grievously. . . . I grieve to find that a man of your quality would have sold yourself for a spy to the enemy of your people. This covetousness is like a canker that eats the iron place where it lies."

Walter stood upright and unmoving as the judge slowly lifted the black cap and set it on his head.

"You shall be had from hence to the place whence you came, there to remain until the day of execution; and from thence you shall be drawn upon a hurdle through the open streets to the place of execution, there to be hanged and cut down alive and your body shall be opened, your heart and bowels plucked out, and your privy members cut off and thrown into the fire before your eyes; then your head shall be stricken off from your body and your body shall be divided into four quarters to be disposed of at the king's pleasure, and God have mercy on your soul."

It did not seem possible that the hideous words of condemnation he had heard so often could apply to himself. He asked that, having regard to the high place he had held in her late majesty's life, he might be granted an honorable death by the ax. It was Lord Thomas Howard, remembering their old comradeship at sea, who promised this, and Cecil added his assurance with tears in his eyes. Whatever Walter felt at the moment, he thanked them and, upright and proud, accompanied the sheriff from the hall.

14 : *"Despair bolts up my doors"*

—Walter Ralegh

James was exasperated. Nothing had gone as he had expected. Sentence had been passed, execution had been fixed for December 13, and now everyone seemed to be on their knees begging him to show mercy to the wretched man, even those who had most disliked him.

"Never any man spoke so well in times past nor would do in the world to come," said Roger Ashton, who had once been dear friend to Essex.

James Hay, one of James's Scots, was declaring to anyone who would listen that "whereas when he saw Sir Walter first, he was so led with the common hatred he would have gone a hundred miles to see him hanged, he would now go a thousand to save his life." Not even the splendid performance of Shakespeare's *As You Like It* stopped James's courtiers from discussing the absorbing topic. Even his host at Wilton House, where he was now staying, the young Earl of Pembroke, was imploring pardon for him.

Cecil and Henry Howard found it maddening that the rival they had sought to destroy, who had gone into the court the most hated man in England, had by his courage and dignity on that single day turned the whole tide of public opinion to his favor. No one believed him guilty, and for the first time men were wondering if the English justice in which they took so much pride was so fine a thing after all. It could not be right, they murmured, that anyone should be condemned on a paper accusation by a man like Cobham, who was not even brought into the court and who at his own trial had shown so poor and miserable a spirit that he disgraced the place where he stood.

Walter, who had been shut up in his cell and permitted no visitors, knew nothing of this. He was suffering intensely from the knowledge that he, an innocent man, had been deliberately and cynically trapped and there was no possible escape. In his first despairing reaction, thinking agonizingly of his wife and son, he had written letter after letter begging for his life. Now he despised himself for it. When the Bishop of Winchester was sent to worm a confession out of him with half promises of mercy, Walter was obstinately and proudly silent. Nothing would induce him to admit what he had not done.

The days crawled by. The intense cold had brought back his fever, and the rheumatic pain in his wounded leg was almost unendurable. In a desperate effort to distract his mind, he turned once again to poetry, something he had not done for many years. The Lord Chief Justice's insults still rang in his mind. "You have been taxed before the world with holding heathenish, blasphemous, atheistical, and prophane opinions," he had said. "Let not anyone persuade you there is no eternity in heaven lest you find an eternity of hell torment." He wondered wearily how many of the men who mocked him had sought as deeply and sincerely for a God to believe in as he had done. He was going, he told himself,

> to Heaven's bribeless hall,
> Where no corrupted voices brawl;
> No conscience molten into gold;
> No forged accuser bought or sold;
> No cause deferred, no vain-spent journey;
> For there Christ is the King's Attorney.

On December 9, hammering outside sounded in his ears all day. They were building the scaffold in the castle courtyard, since Cobham and the others taken with him were to die on the following morning. The time left to him was short. If he could not see Bess, then he must write to her. When he remembered their happy years together, his pen began to race.

"My love I send you, that you may keep it when I am dead. . . . First I send you all the thanks my heart can conceive or my words express for your many troubles and cares taken for me which—though they have not taken effect as you wished— yet my debt is to you never the less; but pay it I never shall in this world."

He was distressed because he had intended to leave her so well provided for and now could do nothing. He had always lived extravagantly and now he was paying for it. Everything he owned would be confiscated by the state.

"Remember your child for his father's sake that chose you and loved you in his happiest times." Then the memory of those imploring letters that had cost him so much to write burned within him and the words poured out. "Get those letters (if it is possible) which I wrote to the Lords wherein I sued for my life. God knows that it was for you and yours that I desired it, but it is true that I disdain myself for begging it. And know it, dear wife, that your son is the child of a true man who despises death and all his misshapen and ugly forms."

It was past midnight, the whole castle was asleep and his single candle was guttering. He wrote the last lines rapidly.

"Time and Death call me away. My true wife, farewell. Bless my poor boy. Pray for me. My true God hold you both in his arms. Yours that was, but now not my own."

But James had planned a little tragicomedy that he kept entirely to himself. The following morning from his window Walter watched the first of the prisoners brought out to die through the drenching rain. The formalities were gone through. The prisoner made his final prayer and knelt, ready to receive the ax's stroke, when there was a loud commotion on the edge of the crowd. Someone was shouting to the executioner to stop and one of the king's Scottish servants came pushing up to the scaffold, waving a letter in his hand.

The high sheriff of Winchester broke the seal. If this was the king's command he must obey it, but his face showed clearly his disgust at his new sovereign's poor sense of humor. The bewildered prisoner was led away. One by one, while the wintry sleet poured down unmercifully, the others were brought out, went through all the dismal preparations, and then were taken away. Even when Cobham came, so swaggering and boastful that the mob hissed him, the same little drama continued. Afterward the wretched victims were gathered together and told that their lives had been spared and their sentence changed to imprisonment for life.

But the scaffold was left in position and for three more days Walter remained in suspense, until on the very morning when he should have died, he was informed that he too was reprieved. On December 16 he was taken back to London and shut up in two tiny, freezing, stone-walled rooms in the Bloody Tower. It would have been so much easier to die. He was an imaginative, passionate man who had lived every moment of his life to the utmost. For five months he had been fighting with all his strength, resilient to every attack, but now the tension snapped. Despair overwhelmed him. The immense vitality that had so often sustained him all but extinguished.

It was like pushing his way through a thick dark blanket to drag himself back to life. Strangely enough, it was sickness that saved him, for it was fear of his death that caused the authorities to grant him a few small liberties. His fighting spirit revived.

Owing to the plague of the previous year, James had not yet made a state entrance into his capital. In March 1604 he rode into London with a great following and was lodged in the Tower of London according to custom. Pardons to prisoners were usually granted at such times of rejoicing, but not to Walter. He was hurriedly removed to the Fleet prison. There were tilts and tournaments, banquets and costly pageants. While James, leaning on the arm of one of his handsome pages, watched a battle between a lion and three great mastiffs, Walter lay in the unspeakable discomfort of a cell dank and evil-smelling from the Fleet sewers. An easy prey to pleurisy, he fought for breath.

The governor of the Fleet prison was in a panic lest Walter should die and as soon as possible he was taken back to the Tower. Sir George Harvey, who like so many others had changed his opinion of his prisoner, sent for a physician. Dr. Turner was very forthright. If they did not want to kill him, he said, then "it were good for him if he were removed from the cold lodging where he lieth unto a warmer."

The Tower of London, from a print published by the Royal Antiquarian Society, based on a 1597 survey
a. Lions' Tower   *b.* Bell Tower   *c.* Beauchamp Tower   *d.* Chapel
e. White Tower   *f.* Jewel House   *g.* Queen's Lodgings   *h.* Queen's Gallery   *i.* Lieutenants' Lodgings   *k.* Bloody Tower   *l.* Traitor's Gate   *m.* Gallows on Tower Hill

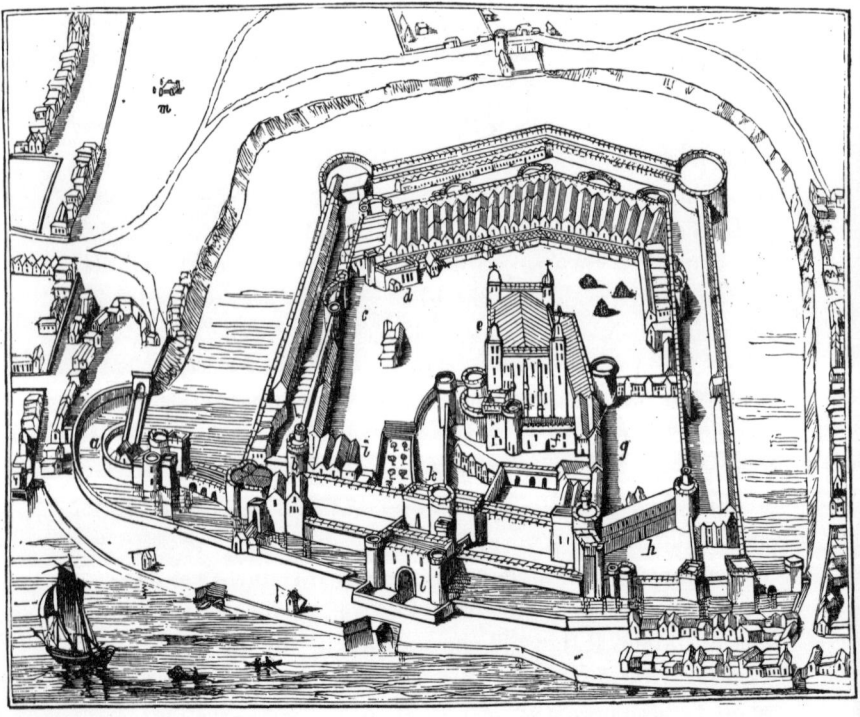

The New York Public Library Picture Collection

It was a bitingly cold spring and even in May there was a damp chill in the Tower. But now Walter was permitted to walk in the lieutenant governor's garden. He could climb stiffly to the rampart and from there see the ships lying at anchor in the Thames. To his right the road ran through the Byward Tower to the royal menagerie, from where, at night, came the lonely roaring of the lions.

His friends had rallied round him. George Carew, Arthur Gorges, Keymis, Tom Hariot were frequent visitors. John Talbot, who had been Wat's tutor, continued still to work for him and willingly shared his captivity. Walter was allowed a chest of his books and was permitted to turn a dilapidated little chicken house in the garden into a laboratory, where he could occupy the endless hours with experiments in medicine and chemistry.

But there were still torturing anxieties. Prisoners had to pay for their own keep. Robert Cecil, driven by pity or conscience, had seen that a little was saved out of the wreckage of Walter's fortune. Sherborne still belonged to the Raleghs, although the fine tapestry hangings from hall and parlor were all sold and Bess had to pawn what silver plate was left to them to provide for their daily living. She and little Wat had come to share his prison with him, which was a comfort to him. But still, to be shut up in two small rooms with a noisy, spoiled boy of eleven was fretting to the raw nerves of a man still sensitive from shock and illness. When Bess became pregnant at the end of May, the prospect of another child after so long and at such a wretched moment of their lives only added to his worries.

"Sorrow rides the ass, prosperity the eagle," he wrote in extreme bitterness when he heard of the honors bestowed on his enemies. Robert Cecil had been created Earl of Salisbury, Henry Howard Earl of Northampton. But Walter was well aware that, even as a prisoner, he was still a thorn in their sides. They had not been able to reduce him to obscurity as they had Cobham and the others. Visitors to the Tower sometimes caught a glimpse of him, and those who dined with the lieutenant governor boasted of their pleasure at finding him a fellow guest. When Carew was born, in February 1605, and was baptized in the Tower chapel, St. Peter ad Vincula, Sir George Harvey not only permitted the baby's father to be present but was there himself.

The privileges did not last, though. Sir William Waad succeeded Harvey as governor, and he had disliked Walter ever since that journey from London to Winchester. It irritated him that the convicted traitor's visiting list was a great deal more distinguished than his own, and he appealed for permission to enforce new and harsh regulations.

He built a high wall so that passersby could no longer see the tall thin figure walking in the garden. Prisoners were forbidden to speak with one another and after five o'clock must be locked into their own rooms. But there was worse to come.

On November 5 the king and the whole country were panic-stricken to discover a Catholic conspiracy to blow up the Houses of Parliament and James himself at the opening of the new session. Guy Fawkes was arrested in the very act of placing the barrels of gunpowder in the cellars. Amid all the interrogations, rackings, and torturings that followed this shocking revelation, the Earl of Northumberland, who was a Catholic, came under suspicion, and he had been Walter's friend. That autumn, down at Sherborne, Bess had caused the house to be cleaned and the armor and weapons in their armory to be scoured and polished. For what reason, his enemies asked one another, unless he was concerned in treason and plotting with the conspirators? Once more he was dragged before the council for questioning and might have laughed at their ridiculous suspicions if he had not been so weary of them.

"I beseech your lordships to remember my services and love to my country and for the love of God not to make me more hateful than ever the earth brought forth any, by suspecting me to be knowing of this unexampled and more than devilish invention," he wrote to them. He was aware now that Cecil and Howard, the very men who had accused him so viciously of accepting a bribe from Spain, were themselves in secret drawing fat pensions from that very country as a reward for the peace they had engineered that summer. He could not restrain his anger and his contempt, and they punished him for it. All his privileges were cut off and he was thrust back once more into the closest confinement—only this time their purpose failed. He accepted it grimly with a half-humorous submission to fate. "The best of men are but the spoils of time," he wrote, "with which childish fortune useth to play—kiss them today and break them tomorrow, and therefore I can lament in myself but a common destiny."

The Gunpowder Plot destroyed his last hope of pardon and liberty, though he never ceased to fight for them. But in the years to come he was to find a new friend, at this moment only a child no older than his little Wat. He was Henry, Prince of Wales, King James's eldest son and the heir to the throne.

15 : *"That Glorious Prince"*

—Walter Ralegh

The winter of 1608 was one of the coldest England had ever known. The wind on the rampart when Walter took his daily walk cut to the bone. The Thames was frozen over from bank to bank, and stalls were set up selling hot pies, sizzling sausages, and fresh-baked cakes. At nightfall great fires blazed and the young people went skimming over the ice on their skates of polished bone. Not that Walter saw much of it. He was shut up in his room at dusk.

The deadly monotony of life in the Tower had been eased a little by the detention of Northumberland for his supposed connection with the Gunpowder Plot. Still fabulously wealthy, the Wizard Earl took a certain malicious pleasure in turning the Martin Tower upside down, cutting new windows, refurnishing it, and bringing in his own cook and servants. With him came a vast library, and Tom Hariot to help him with his scientific studies. Prisoners were not allowed to meet, but Hariot went between the earl and Walter, carrying books and exchanging notes on all kinds of experiments. To Sir William Waad's mean, suspicious eyes, it looked as if the famous "School of Night" were starting up again in the Tower.

Reports from the world outside reached Walter at intervals. It seemed that James was still making up for the years of poverty in Scotland. Lavish and riotous entertainments followed one another at the court. The king was quarreling with his Parliament and driving Robert Cecil frantic by appeals for more money while he neglected affairs of state in his passion for hunting. He had been given a cheetah by the Duke of Savoy, and the lithe, sinuous creature could outrun even the swiftest hare.

With so little else to occupy his time, Walter spent long hours in his shed-laboratory distilling medicines. "I think the Indians in Guiana taught me more about their secret remedies than anyone," he told George Carew once. Soon everyone at court was talking about Walter's magical elixir and how it could cure all manner of sickness and fever. Nonetheless, Walter was surprised when George Carew, who had been made Baron Carew of Clopton, brought him news of James's queen, Anne of Denmark. She was suffering from a feverish ague and was eager to try a dose of the famous medicine. Would Walter give him a phial to bring to the queen?

Still young and frivolous, the queen wasn't happy with her husband's interests and way of life. She loved to act in the court masques, costly entertainments of music, poetry, and dancing. In the *Masque of Blackness* she and her ladies had painted their faces black and, dressed in blue and silver and shimmering with jewels, floated onto the stage in a shell glimmering like mother-of-pearl. She, too, firmly believed in Walter's innocence. When her brother, King Christian, had visited England, he had asked James to let Walter return to Denmark with him as his admiral, but the request was refused. James was afraid of what Walter might do if he were free in Europe.

Arthur Gorges was attached to the staff of the young Prince of Wales and told Walter how utterly different Henry was from his father. Intelligent, a fine athlete, keenly interested in affairs of state and studying the strategy of war, he had a most hearty dislike of the flattering men the king surrounded himself with. Especially, he had no use for Robert Carr, the new favorite. Carr was a young Scot, handsome, vigorous, and emptyheaded, who had first attracted the king's notice when he broke a leg jousting in a court tournament. James loved his children but found them disappointing. Henry was independent, rebellious, always ready to criticize and argue with his father; Elizabeth, two years younger, adored her brother and followed his lead in every like and dislike; baby Charles was only eight, sickly and backward, with an awkward stammer and such weak legs that he had not been able to walk until he was nearly five. Most people did not expect him to live.

A lad like Robbie Carr, who owed everything to James, whom he could spoil and favor, meant a great deal to the king, whose childhood had been so lonely and so starved of affection. What he never seemed to realize was how the young man took advantage of his generosity, how greedy and arrogant he soon became, and in consequence how hated he was by Prince Henry and the English courtiers.

One of the prince's absorbing interests was the navy. He watched Walter's old *Ark Royal* being refitted and was forever pressing his father to build new ships. "You are a man after his

James I

Henry, Prince of Wales.
Painting by P. Van Somer

own heart," said Gorges jestingly when he visited Walter one day in January.

After Gorges had gone, Walter looked at the ship he was constructing, something else to occupy him during the long candle-lit evenings. On an impulse, he picked up his pen and wrote down all those principles of shipbuilding that he had tried and tested himself. When the letter was done and dispatched to the prince, he turned back again to the great work that he had set himself to accomplish.

Once long ago in the happy days at Sherborne, he had thought "to write the story of all ages past," but then his life had been filled with action. He had not the leisure for such a formidable task. Now with so many tedious hours to fill, he was fascinated by the prospect. The story of man from the Creation—David, Solomon, Alexander, Hannibal, Caesar—the heroic names unrolled like a panorama of glory, courage, ambition, and disaster. It gripped his imagination so that the old powerful energy revived. To Bess's alarm, he cut down on sleep, reading early and late, begging his friends for books and ancient documents and manuscripts, forgetting that he was a man of fifty-four, heavily restricted, without the health and strength he had once possessed.

His son had been causing him a great deal of anxiety. Prison was no place to bring up a lively, intelligent boy. There were no suitable companions and he had made friends with some of the wilder sons of Tower officials. Walter had always felt very close to Wat and had never treated him harshly as so many fathers did their sons, but now the high-spirited lad was always getting in some foolish scrape or other. Walter was at his wit's end and finally decided to send him to Oxford, though he was barely fourteen. Sometimes he felt he took more pleasure in the three-year-old Carew playing about his feet as he wrote and studied.

"That Glorious Prince" : 183

It was April before the ice melted and the green spears of daffodils appeared in the governor's garden. At Sherborne the chestnut avenue would be bursting into fat brown buds. There would be yellow drifts of primroses and clumps of violets in the woods. The water birds would be nesting on the shores of the lake. He never thought he would have longed so much to see such simple things. Like a black shadow was the ever-present fear that Sherborne might be taken from them. Years ago, before his trial, he had made over the estate to his son, so it should have been safe, but a careless lawyer's clerk had omitted a clause in copying the deed. It meant that Sherborne still belonged to him and therefore the state could claim it at any time. It was the one thing that made Bess, distracted by her many anxieties, turn on him with bitter reproaches, accusing him of reckless neglect in not examining the deed more closely, crying out that he thought only of himself and cared nothing for her and his sons.

In an agony of distress, for if their love for one another was destroyed, there would indeed be nothing left to him, he humbled himself once more, and wrote imploringly to Robert Cecil for his help. The king promised reluctantly that Sherborne should be kept in trust for his wife and children, but Walter knew how uncertain such a promise was. If but one of James's greedy Scots should cast an envious eye on it, it could be lost to the Raleghs forever.

With the summer there came an unexpected visitor, whom at first Walter greeted with a wary reserve despite what Arthur Gorges had said. Prince Henry was sixteen, tall and slim, with light-brown hair and a frank, friendly manner. He had admired his father's prisoner for a long time, had read every word of his trial, and had formed his own opinion.

"I have come to ask your advice," he said with an engaging

charm when he came informally to him in his cell. "I would be very clear when next I go to Phineas Pett at Deptford. He remembers you very well, Sir Walter."

Phineas was the son of old Peter Pett and as brilliant a builder of ships as ever his father had been. The prince's questions were intelligent. From the time he was twelve he had sailed a small yacht of his own and was not ignorant of seamanship.

"I understand all the points you listed in your letter to me," he said. "A well-found ship should be strongly built, swift in sail, stout-sided—but why do you insist that it should be small and low in the water? Against a heavy galleon it would surely carry no weight."

"It is not the size that counts, Your Highness, it is the ability to maneuver quickly and easily, to be able to take advantage of every puff of wind. We proved that when we fought the Armada and even more so at Cadiz. To clap ships one against the other is as out of date as it is clumsy. A small ship can turn twice and deliver a double broadside from her guns before the heavier galleon has lumbered into a half-turn. A fleet of only twenty would have the advantage on the open sea of a hundred of slower sailing."

It was the first of many visits. The boy's belief in his innocence warmed him as nothing else had done since his condemnation. The prince in turn was fascinated by this man who talked to him of the great days of Elizabeth, of Guiana, of Virginia, of those dreams of empire that still occupied his thoughts. He had kept in touch with every expedition that had set sail in these last few years. In 1606 Ralegh Gilbert, Humphrey's son, and Algernon Percy, the brother of the Wizard Earl, had gone to Virginia; in the same year the brothers Leigh had set out for Guiana, and they had all come to him in the Tower for his advice. The charts he spread before the prince's eyes were marked with every new discovery, and his lively charm of manner made James's councilors seem heavy and dull by comparison.

Already Henry was on bad terms with his father. They disagreed about almost everything. The boy, straightforward and very serious, despised the frivolous court with its popinjay favorites and idle luxury; and the king, jealous of his son's growing popularity with the ordinary people, was irritated that he should disobey him by seeking out the man who should have been long forgotten.

For five years Walter had been learning the bitter lessons of imprisonment: the ill-health, the humiliations, the poverty that is an "imprisonment of the mind, a vexation of every worthy spirit," as he wrote savagely. He still obstinately maintained his innocence. Even to gain his freedom, he would not deny it. But in the long lonely hours he had learned to know himself better. "Men are the causes of their own miseries as I was of mine," he wrote. The experience of others teaches you nothing, you have to walk the hard path of your own follies to find the inner self. Yet he was not soured. Despite everything, the keen mind still longed to be of use in the world, and now suddenly in the young prince he had found a purpose. This was his future king, the heir to the crown of England. The friendship between them grew warmer. Henry brought his problems to Walter and eagerly listened to his advice. Walter began to instruct him in statecraft, dipping deep into his own experience.

James was furious. He complained to his ministers, but there was little they could do. It seemed impossible to silence Walter. Everything he wrote reflected upon the extravagance of the court and on the shabby men who ruled England as if she were a third-rate power existing on the edge of Europe only by the favor of France and Spain. The prince found his views absorbing and took to quoting them at all times.

"Sir Walter has told me of Queen Elizabeth," he said one day at a council meeting. "How she would set the reason of a good man before the greatest councilor she had because she was the queen of small people as well as great. In those days one English ship could have compelled forty foreigners to strike sail, and now even the Netherlanders can make us turn tail and run."

It was the same clear outspoken voice coming from the Tower like a ghost from the past. When Henry Howard would have protested, Henry turned on him with contempt. "Only a man like my father would keep such a bird in a cage!"

Walter's enemies looked for a way to punish him, and it was not difficult to find. The handsome eyes of Robbie Carr had fallen on Sherborne, and to please him James forgot his solemn promise. Cecil was ordered to arrange its transfer. He knew, none better, how much it meant to Walter and how Bess clung to it as the sole inheritance left to their two sons. But Walter was not the only one to suffer from the king's whims, thought Cecil sourly. He himself had been forced to hand over to James Theobolds, the beloved house that had been Lord Burghley's pride, and all he had been given in exchange was the crumbling royal palace of Hatfield. The fine new mansion he was building there was digging deep into his own wealth. Let the Raleghs manage how they could.

Long afterward Carew was to write bitterly how as a small child he remembered seeing his mother kneel on the gravel path at Hampton Court begging James to have pity and save her and her children from ruin and beggary. The king pushed past her with his shambling walk, muttering in his thick Scots: "I maun have it for Carr, I maun have it for Carr!"

Driven beyond herself, Bess implored Walter to write to Carr himself. But how could he beg favor from this upstart boy who lorded it about the court by the king's favor? Was there no end to the humiliations forced on him?

"Must I go on my knees for you again?" he asked in torment, and Bess, the tears running down her face, lashed out at him. "I can kneel and be mocked by the whole insolent court while you stay here and keep your pride untouched."

He did as she asked, but the dignity of his appeal did not touch the selfish heart of the young favorite. Sneeringly he read the letter to the king: "There remains nothing with me but the bare name of life . . . and for yourself, sir, seeing your day is but now in the dawn and mine come to the evening . . . I beseech you not to begin your first buildings upon the ruins of the innocent."

James did not want to listen. Everything about Walter irritated him—his pride, his independence, his refusal to accept the slights put upon him, even so little a thing as his smoking. In 1604 the king had published his *Counterblast to Tobacco*. It was a custom, he wrote, "loathesome to the eye, hateful to the nose, harmful to the brain, dangerous to the lungs, and in the black stinking fume thereof nearest resembling the horrible Stygian smoke of the pit that is bottomless." It had not stopped a single one of his subjects from smoking their pipes when and where they wished.

The long legal argument over Sherborne lasted for months and ended in defeat for Walter. The estate where he had dreamed of spending his old age with his sons and his grandsons was gone forever. Bess was allowed compensation and a small pension. It was not a quarter of what the place was worth and very irregularly paid, but it was all they had to live on. One by one, their remaining possessions would have to be sold. It nearly broke Bess's heart to part with the last few jewels that had been Walter's gifts to her.

It was Prince Henry who finally tried to do something for them. In great anger, he stormed into his father's presence protesting that a house of such beauty as Sherborne should remain in the possession of the crown and loudly demanding it for himself. James could never stand up to his tempestuous son. He gave in. Carr was given a huge sum of money in its place and Henry held Sherborne in trust for the man he was determined that his father should pardon before very long.

Despite his father's wishes, the prince refused to give up his visits to the Tower. Walter's *History of the World* was being expanded to please him. He was not a bookish boy, but when he read the manuscript and discussed it with Walter, he seemed to be listening to the history of his own times in the story of the Israelites, the Persians, and the Greeks. Every now and again, when some event reminded Walter of his own experiences, he would enliven the narrative with personal anecdotes that brought the past to vivid life.

In 1611, when Henry was seventeen, James urged him to wed the daughter of the half-Spanish Duke of Savoy. The prince argued violently with his father and came hurrying to Walter, begging for his help. "I will not have two religions in my bed," he said. Walter, who could never remember that his greatest safety lay in keeping quiet, spoke out boldly. He pointed out the folly of such an unpopular match, which, if the prince should die, would not only put England in the power of Catholic princes but could lead to civil war. The heretics burned at the stake in Mary Tudor's time were not yet forgotten. His arguments were too clear and reasonable to be refuted, and the king was so angry that Cecil himself came to the Tower, sternly rebuking Walter for influencing the prince against his father. Walter forgot caution and answered sharply. Once more they punished him, banishing Bess from his side and thrusting him back into close imprisonment for three winter months.

The cold brought back his fever, but it did not rob him of the prince's affection. By Christmas of 1612 Henry would be of age, and "then, Sir Walter," he said, his hazel eyes glowing with pleasure, "my father has promised that you will be pardoned and set free." For a few hopeful months it seemed to Walter that fortune might be favoring him at last.

When Cecil had visited him in the Tower to convey the king's anger, Walter had been shocked by his appearance. Only forty-eight, he looked an old man, his face haggard, his eyes sunk in brown hollows of weariness. Walter was not really surprised to hear a few months later in May that Cecil had died suddenly on his way back from Bath, where he had gone to seek a cure in the hot sulfur springs. The crude verses of the street ballads found their way even into Walter's prison:

> Not Robin Goodfellow, nor Robin Hood,
> But Robin the Devil who never did good.
> Here lieth Robin Crookback, unjustly reckoned
> A Richard the Third, he was Judas the Second.

Walter could feel no pity for the man who had destroyed the friendship between them but he knew that, in his own way, Cecil had served England well. He dropped the vile broadsheet into the fire.

In the autumn Frederick, Elector of the Palatine in Germany, small, dark, and very shy, arrived in England for his marriage with the Princess Elizabeth. His family were not rich, and he gasped at the magnificence of the English court. He felt very insignificant standing beside the tall Prince of Wales as he bent to kiss the hand of his exquisite bride. At fifteen Elizabeth already had all the charm and beauty that were to win her the name of "Queen of Hearts" and Frederick had quickly fallen in love with her.

The Protestant match was a popular one, and public rejoicing was great. There were tournaments, banquets, extravagant masques, and a new play by Shakespeare, brought back from retirement at Stratford-on-Avon for the occasion. In *The Tempest* he drew a picture of James as a learned royal magician and his daughter as a fairy-tale princess. There was a tremendous storm to remind everyone of the latest expedition to Virginia, in which Walter had invested a little money and which had been blown off course by a hurricane and landed up in the Bermudas.

It seemed as if the gaiety would never end, until Prince Henry suddenly fainted at a banquet and his doctors in a panic got him to bed. He had been suffering from fever but had made light of it and rashly gone swimming in the Thames after an afternoon of tennis. They were making a fuss about nothing, he said, but he grew worse, and anxiety deepened. Elizabeth begged to see her brother but was forbidden for fear of infection. The queen, remembering her own sickness, sent an urgent request for Walter's medicine. He dispatched it at once.

The physicians refused to give it to the prince until they had tried every remedy and the boy was unconscious. After some of the Privy Council had swallowed a draught of it themselves and were none the worse, they administered it to the dying prince. It brought him briefly out of his coma; he could even speak and his fever had gone—but they had waited too long. His weakness was too great. A few hours later he was dead.

So much money had been spent that the marriage feast had to go on, though the bride varied between hysterical laughter and frantic tears and her wedding gown was of black satin and silver in mourning for her loved brother. England wept for the loss of the popular young heir, and James ran away from his fear of sickness and death, hunting the red deer from morning to night. Sherborne was handed back to Robert Carr and the promise of Walter's pardon so solemnly given to the prince was conveniently forgotten with his death.

Christmas came and went and Walter drove himself to work to numb his thoughts. He was bringing the first part of his *History* to a conclusion and knew now that he would write no more.

"It has pleased God to take that glorious prince out of the world to whom it was directed," he wrote in the concluding paragraph. Then he threw down his pen and got up, pacing up and down the small square room; he knew every inch, every ugly crack in the stone walls, every ridge in the uneven floor. He missed the eager intelligent boy who had been both pupil and friend and who for four years had been as close to him as his own son. At fifty-eight it does not seem possible that eighteen can die. And, of course, with him vanished the hope of freedom that had been so near.

But Walter could not stay idle for long and soon he spread out the old Guiana charts. A short time before, he had written a desperate letter to the queen imploring her intercession with her husband to let him go to Guiana, promising that he would leave his wife and children as pledges of his good faith and that Lady Ralegh would give herself to death if he tried to escape and failed to return.

Bess had wept when he told her of it, distressed that he should still be willing to risk so much for an impossible dream, even though she knew that he would never desert her, that only death would prevent his coming back.

His long finger traced the old route up the Orinoco. There was gold in Guiana, he was certain of it. He had discussed it with Lawrence Keymis night after night; the ore he had brought back had been retested here in the Tower and the proof was there. Gold was the one lure that might tempt the king to set him free, he thought, with a certain contempt. With Cecil gone, there was a chance, a slight hope. It was a project the difficulties of which he dare not admit, a dream that during the long years of imprisonment had become dangerously near to obsession.

16 : "His Last Dream"

—Sir Thomas Wilson

A wild March wind was whipping up the waters of the Thames and ruffling the feathers of the ravens strutting on Tower Green when Walter walked through his narrow door for the last time, a prisoner no longer. He had been released so that he might make arrangements for his voyage to Guiana. He was still under sentence of death. He was forbidden the court, he must not approach the queen or appear in any public assembly whatsoever, but on that bright morning in 1616 all that seemed of very small importance to a man who had paced the same few yards of graveled path for thirteen years. He went immediately to the little house Bess had taken in Broad Street in the city of London, his mind running back over the four years that had dragged so wearily after the prince's death.

His *History of the World* had been published in 1614 and

was an immediate success with everyone except the king. He had known he must be careful. "He who walks too closely at the heel of truth is liable to be kicked in the teeth," he had written once, but truth was important to him, and he was too daringly critical for James, who believed in the divine right of kings to do as they wish. "He is too saucy in censuring princes," James said, impatiently flicking over the pages: what right had Ralegh, a disgraced prisoner, to put his own name and portrait on the title page?

He sent out an order to the publishers for the book to be withdrawn, but the order was never carried out. Public demand was too great. A second edition had been issued and soon there would be a third. There was satisfaction in knowing that no royal disapproval could belittle his achievement, but Walter had not continued with it. The strong urge to work on it had died with the prince. Perhaps when he was really old, he might complete it as his last task on earth, but now he was young again, he was free, and before him lay the fulfillment he had never lost sight of in all those imprisoned years. At long last he would redeem his promise to the Indians in Guiana. He would have to find the gold, of course, since that was the reason the king was allowing him to go, but the vision in his own mind was far greater than that, though he dare not express it too openly.

No one could have foreseen how strangely events would turn to his favor. Robbie Carr, brought to the highest peak of ambition as Earl of Somerset, had made a disastrous marriage with an unscrupulous woman who had involved him in charges of witchcraft and murder. His fall was as spectacular as his rise. Walter's release from prison had come months earlier than he expected, since his rooms in the Tower were required for Carr and his wife. Henry Howard, the old enemy, had died suddenly. Sir Ralph Winwood, who had been appointed Secretary of State in place of Cecil, was violently opposed to the Spanish alliance and argued daily in the council against the king's intention of marrying the young Prince Charles to the Infanta of Spain.

Then James had never had the knack of managing his Parliament as Elizabeth had done. Obtaining money from them was like squeezing blood out of a stone. He began to wonder if there might be something after all in Walter's hare-brained scheme for finding gold in Guiana. Finally, his interest was caught by a new young man pushed forward by the anti-Spanish party, the strikingly handsome George Villiers, who had the face of the martyred St. Stephen in the painting that hung in the king's closet.

It was the right moment at last. Urged by his friends, Walter sent a bribe to Villiers, and the young man used his new influence with the king, who listened, was tempted, still refused to grant a pardon, but half reluctantly, half hopefully, signed the order of release.

Walter's very first action was to commission a new ship from Phineas Pett. The *Destiny* he called her, with a bold thrust at Fate. He had endured her buffetings for long enough. Now he would be master of his own future. Then, out of sheer delight in his freedom, he walked about the streets he had known so well, taking eleven-year-old Carew with him.

So much had changed. The roads were thronged with the new carriages that everyone seemed to be using now instead of taking a horse. In Islington, where he had shot wild duck, the New River had been cut, bringing piped water to the city houses. The water carriers were furious at losing their livelihood. They spread the rumor that the pipes would burst and everyone would be drowned, but more and more people turned gladly to the wonderful new convenience. The frontage of Walter's own Durham House had been turned by Cecil into a double arcade of shops called the New Exchange, a monument to the power of gold that seemed to dominate this new age. Houses had sprung up where he had remembered open fields and cows grazing. "You will have to walk as far as Islington to hear the cuckoo now," he was told.

One morning he went to Westminster Abbey and, looking down at the new sculptured effigy, saw again the aquiline nose and high cheekbones of the woman he had loved and served. Elizabeth's tomb was mounted on four lions, the black pillars supporting a stone canopy with the arms of England blazing around it in gold, scarlet, and blue. He stood so lost in memories that, though Carew longed to question him, he did not dare. His mother had told him often enough of his father's former splendor, and now, looking at the tall thin figure still so upright and elegant, he saw him for a moment as he must have been and felt his heart swell with pride.

Although he was barred from the court, Walter was invited almost everywhere else. He dined at all the great houses and supped at the Mermaid, still the haunt of poets, playwrights, and actors. Francis Beaumont summed up those exciting evenings full of talk and laughter:

>What things have we seen
>Done at the Mermaid! heard words that hath been
>So nimble, and so full of subtle flame
>As if that everyone from whence they came
>Had meant to put his whole wit in a jest.

Some faces were missing. Will Shakespeare had died that April; Edward Alleyn had retired to Dulwich and founded a

National Gallery of Ireland

Sir Walter in his later years

school there for poor boys; but Ben Jonson was still writing and full of grumbles about Wat. Walter had persuaded him to accompany his son to Paris as his tutor when Wat came down from Oxford, and the lad had played trick after trick on him, even getting him dead drunk on one occasion and trundling him along the streets on a handcart. Walter was proud of his bold handsome son, but his madcap behavior still caused him anxiety. The boy had recently picked a quarrel with another young man, swords had been drawn, and blood spilled. Since duels were forbidden, there was nothing to do but cross the Channel and fight it out in Holland. Fortunately the English ambassador stepped in and prevented the duel, for Walter's sake. Now Wat was home again and wild to go with him to Guiana.

One day that summer, just for pure pleasure, Walter, his two sons, and Phineas Pett sailed down the river and around to Dover in a new pinnace. Carew begged to go to Guiana too, but was told he must stay and care for his mother. It was disappointing, but his father's smile, his hand on his shoulder, made him feel grownup and responsible. For Walter it was sheer ecstasy to stand on his own deck, even though it was only the tiny pinnace, to feel the movement of the sea and taste the salt on his lips. He was sixty-two, but he never thought of himself as old. He had put the weariness and sickness of the Tower behind him.

All his friends were urging him not to risk his life in this mad gamble. It was crazy, they said, when he was still under sentence of death. It was more than twenty years since his first voyage and things had changed. How could he be sure of finding the gold mine after all this time? The Spaniards had established a fortified town close to his route, and the new Spanish ambassador, Count Gondomar, was poisoning James's mind about Walter every day.

Walter would not listen to them. If he did what they asked, if he scraped together the last money left to him and bought a pardon from the king, what sort of future lay before him? Nothing but a few years of poverty and obscurity. That was what he found so unbearable. His mind had always leaped ahead. He could not give up before he had made one more bid to realize his lifelong dream of establishing an English empire overseas. It was one last grand gesture and if he failed, then he failed. But now in the exultation of freedom he was determined to succeed.

However, he did show some caution. He went to see Francis Bacon, who was Lord Keeper of the Great Seal, Lord Chancellor, Baron Verulam, and Viscount St. Albans, and possessed the finest legal mind in England. Walter asked him frankly if he should gather together every penny and obtain the king's official pardon before he sailed.

"Money is the knee-timber of your voyage, Sir Walter," was Bacon's reply. "Spare your gold . . . for upon my life, you have a sufficient pardon for all that is past already, the king having under his great seal made you admiral and given you power of martial law."

That meant that in case of rebellion or mutiny among his men he had the power of life and death whether at sea or on land.

"Your commission," Bacon assured him, "is as good a pardon for all former offenses as the law of England can afford you."

Such an opinion from such an authority was surely good enough. "You have lifted a burden from me," said Walter thankfully.

The two thin elderly men, so alike in their keen searching intellects, were completely different in temperament. Walter was bold, audacious, and reckless; Bacon, cautious and secretive. As they continued to stroll and talk together in the gardens of Gray's Inn, Bacon asked casually, "What will you do if after all this expenditure you miss the gold mine?"

And Walter, who could never remember to guard his tongue, said jestingly, "Why, we will look for the Spanish treasure fleet, of course."

"But then you would be pirates," said Bacon, a little shocked.

"Oh no, who ever heard of men being pirates for millions!" was Walter's laughing reply. Not that he was seriously considering plundering the Spanish treasure ships, tempting though it was; he had realized that such an exploit was twenty years too late.

The *Destiny* was launched in December and it became the fashion to visit her as she lay in the Thames and, if you were lucky, catch a glimpse of her famous admiral. The queen longed to do so, but James forbade it. He had been behaving very strangely of late. He was so terrified of assassination that he had a barricade of bedsteads put around the one he slept in as protection against an intruder. It worried Walter that he could not meet the king face to face. When he and Keymis had restudied the latest charts of Guiana, he had realized that they might well have to fight the Spaniards in order to reach the mine, and England was at peace with Spain. Anxious to safeguard himself, he had suggested to Sir Ralph Winwood that they might persuade France to lend a party of troops, who would act as escort and leave the English free to advance to the mine. He wrote to James warning him of his problem, and Winwood assured him that his difficulties were understood.

What neither Walter nor Winwood nor anyone knew was that the king had handed over to the persistent Gondomar every detail of the expedition: the number of ships, their armaments, and the ports of call; and had made a solemn promise that if only one Spaniard were harmed, Walter would be sent in chains to Spain to be hanged in the marketplace of Madrid.

Gondomar was a curious character. Unlike the usual proud, reserved Spaniard, he could act the buffoon, amusing James with sly jokes and a chuckling good humor; but he knew exactly how to play upon the king's half-timid, half-aggressive temperament, and he used his skill brilliantly. Spain had a long score to settle with Walter Ralegh, "that old pirate bred under the English virago and by her fleshed in Spanish blood and ruin," he wrote to his master.

It had not been easy for Walter to find sufficient funds to equip the expedition. Every penny they had was going into it. Bess sold the last small property left to her, and it distressed Walter that he had to leave her with nothing but the irregularly paid pension from the king.

In March 1617, just before he sailed the *Destiny* down to Plymouth, a distinguished party of friends gathered on ship to bid him farewell. Two of the guests, the Earls of Arundel and Pembroke, who had given him loyal support, took him aside to tell him that they had pledged on their honor to the king that, whatever happened, he would not try to escape. It warmed him to know that he still had friends who believed in his integrity. There and then he gave them a solemn promise that, short of death, nothing would prevent him fulfilling what he had vowed to the king.

In Devon he was greeted with a rousing reception. At the

grand banquet given by the mayor of Plymouth, Carew felt as if his heart would burst with pride and happiness. He could not understand why his mother sat with tears in her eyes as she watched her husband once more seated in the place of honor and welcomed with admiration and respect.

Walter was still troubled by the necessities of his company. It had not been easy to find responsible captains to sail with him. He had to borrow from friends and pledge his credit. Bess had to enter into a bond to pay Captain Pennington's grocery bills and settle the raffish Captain Whitney's debts. It was summer before the ships were fully equipped and Walter issued his *Orders to the Fleet*, clear and humane—every order, however strict, accompanied by the reason for it. He had never demanded blind obedience. His sailors were encouraged to be reasoning, intelligent free men, not slaves.

On June 12, Bess stood on the quayside at Plymouth and watched them sail, thirteen ships with the *Destiny* flying the admiral's flag. She had supported him every step of the way, trying hard not to show her fear and anxiety. "Love that gives, that sticks at nothing," he had said tenderly. Now he was gone, taking her dearly loved son with him, and there was nothing to do but wait—and pray—for his safe return.

17 : "My Name hath lived among them"

—Walter Ralegh

It was September already and they had only reached the Canary Islands. Walter paused in writing up his journal for the day. Through the windows of his cabin he could see the sun sparkling on the water and the foam of their wake streaming behind them as the *Destiny* scudded before a fresh breeze. But by the time they reached Cape Verde, they would be full in the hurricane season, and he dreaded the battering they might have to endure. They had sailed from Plymouth into summer storms so fierce that the inexperienced sailors, shaken with seasickness, had been almost useless. They had had to take refuge in Kinsale harbor, and there he had been forced to remain for seven long weeks waiting for a favorable wind.

In some ways it had been pleasant. Lord Boyle, who had bought his Irish estates, had entertained him royally in what had once been his own castle of Lismore. He took Walter hawking along the Blackwater, where he had gone fishing with Edmund Spenser, who now lay buried in Westminster Abbey. While Wat enjoyed himself flirting with his host's pretty daughters, Walter had listened to Lord Boyle, who tried hard to point out the wisdom of making a bid for freedom while he had the chance. France would welcome him if only to spite James, he said, or he could always go to King Christian in Denmark.

It was true. It was what everyone seemed to expect him to do, but if he had wanted to trade his service to a foreign country, he could have done it years ago before his trial. What lay closest to his heart was the determination to wipe away the stain of traitor, regain the dignity of a free man, and prove that he still had it in him to give something to the country that had always had his love.

When the wind changed and Walter readied his ships at last, Lord Boyle heaped him with gifts: a hundred oxen, a store of biscuit, money, a thirty-two-gallon cask of the whiskey he still detested. Now that Ireland was peaceful, he was making a good profit out of the lands that Walter had tilled and planted.

On August 19 the ships set out again. Walter had good friends with him: his nephew George Ralegh; Lawrence Keymis; Captain Sam King, who had sailed so many of his ships in the old days; John Talbot, close to him all the years in the Tower. He enjoyed their company and yet was conscious of deep loneliness. It seemed that imprisonment had set a barrier between him and the rest of the world. His journal was written only for himself. There he could record the sudden sparkling showers, the starlit skies, the rainbows that arched across the horizon, the moonlight washing over the deck at midnight. It all came fresh and miraculous to a man who had been shut at curfew behind thick stone walls.

But there were evenings when they all supped with him in his cabin and discussed the coming trip up the Orinoco. Relaxed and happy, master in his own ship, he would forget the need for caution and talk openly of what Winwood had said about fighting the Spaniards, even about that rash notion of capturing the treasure fleet. Without his intending it, the rumor ran all around the fleet that he would not object to a little piracy. Captain Bayley certainly thought so, and Walter was forced to prevent him plundering four French ships he had stopped. In a rage, the captain sailed off on his own account.

At the island of Lanzarote in the Canaries, Walter's request for provisions had been treated with open contempt by the Spanish governor, and he had a stormy battle with his officers, whose only desire was to punish the unfriendly island. They could not see as he could how dangerous it was to raise a finger against Spain or how much damage it would do to the English merchantmen already moored in the harbor.

Captain Bayley had raced back to England intent on revenge. One morning Gondomar forced himself into the king's presence shouting "Pirate! Pirate!" full in his face. James was upset; he never knew whether Gondomar was joking or deadly serious. It was George Carew who demanded that this rascal of a captain should be closely questioned. Bayley gave way under cross-examination, confessed his lies, and was clapped into prison. Then dispatches arrived from the Englishmen in Lanzarote praising Walter's patience under extreme provocation. Even at the island of Gomera, where he had been greeted with a hail of musket shot, he had not retaliated, keeping strict control and only guarding his men with his guns when they went ashore to fill the water casks. But in England Bayley's lies still clung. It was too easy to believe them, too many people to say "No smoke without a fire!"

Walter had other more serious enemies to fight just then than slanders back in England. When they sailed away from Gomera toward Cape Verde, they met the full force of hurricanes that drove them off course and drenched them in cold salt water even in their cabins. Worst of all, a strange sickness fell upon them, a burning fever that ran through all the ships. Forty died on the *Destiny* alone, among them some of his best men and, to his great sorrow, his faithful friend John Talbot.

They moved out of the belt of storms into a breathless heat. There was no wind to fill the sails and they lay becalmed under a pitiless sun. Their water was running short. The leather buckets cracked in the heat without a drop of rain or dew in them to cool the men's parched throats. For two days they were engulfed in a darkness so thick they had to steer by candle-light and it took all Walter's charm and authority to soothe the superstitious fears of his seamen. Then the unnatural calm broke into a raging gale so unexpected and so violent that it caught them totally unprepared.

On October 30 Walter was almost thrown out of his bed by the force of the gust that hit the ship. He heard the shouts of the men as they struggled to shorten the sails and he rushed up on deck to take control. All that black night the ship bucketed and dipped in a savage sea. In weather like this there was no time to worry about the rest of the fleet. Each ship had to fight her own battle. It was full day before the wind eased. The storm began to blow itself out and he could glimpse *Star*, the *John and Francis*, the *Flying Joan*, and the others still riding the sea.

His face strained with fatigue, his clothes sodden, he stumbled down to his cabin, but the damage to his health had been done.

He caught a violent chill that turned to a fever and was more desperately ill than he had ever been in his whole life. Every few hours they had to strip his wet shirt from him. He could eat nothing, only drink lemon juice squeezed into the thick tepid water to still his raging thirst. In the stifling cabin he lay sweating for a fortnight, struggling to keep control while his mind wandered in delirious dreams.

On November 11 the man in the crow's nest called "Land ho," and Wat came to tell him that they had sighted the mainland of South America. Three days later they sailed into the harbor of Cayenne. Now was the critical moment. Twenty years before, he had won the affection of the Indians by kindness and tolerance, but since then they had been treated with the utmost cruelty by Spain, and England had not provided the protection he had promised. It would be little wonder if they rejected him now. He sent Keymis ashore to contact the Indian chief and waited. He was still far too weak to walk or even stand. They carried him up to the deck, but even under the rough sailcloth awning the heat was intense and there was no breeze to blow away the reek of sick men unable to move.

At sunset Keymis returned and with him came the Indians. They swarmed onto his deck, piling baskets of fruit, cassava bread, and fresh meat around his feet. Then the chief came himself. He was the boy he had taken to England, the son of Topiawari, who had returned to claim his inheritance on the death of his father. He was bowing and smiling as he held out a basket of pineapples. Walter was touched that they should have remembered so small a thing about him as his liking for the "princess of fruits."

It was a relief to be on shore in an open tent with a cool wind blowing through it. After a few days he was able to eat a little of the roasted fish, the fine fresh bread, and the sharp, delicious pineapple. Very slowly he began to gather a little strength. A Dutch ship in the harbor was returning to Europe. He took the opportunity to write cheerfully to Bess, making light of his sickness, telling her that Wat was in splendid health and that he was confident that now all would go well. "To tell you that I might be here king of the Indians were a vanity; but my name hath lived among them. . . . All offer to obey me."

As Walter sealed the letter, he prayed that what he had written would prove true. Never, even in his most depressed moments, had he imagined that he would not be able to lead the expedition up the Orinoco himself, but when by the end of November he still could not walk more than a few steps without assistance, he knew it was impossible. For a sick man to undertake so long and dangerous a journey would be madness. But so many men had died that there was no one on whom he could absolutely rely to take his place.

Keymis had the advantage of knowing the country. He was loyal and trustworthy, but he had always lacked the self-confidence of a leader. But there was no help for it. He must be in command. George Ralegh was capable but young. He could lead the soldiers, with Wat as captain. About his son Walter hesitated for a long time. He was popular with the men. They liked his dash and spirit. They would follow him anywhere, but God only knew what reckless action he might rush into without his father to restrain him. Yet to forbid his going would so hit at his young pride that the boy would never forgive him. Walter had to let him go.

He recruited every man fit enough to make the journey, leaving himself only sick and convalescent crews. They had all been alarmed at tales of Spanish aggression. They knew their leader went in peril of his life. On the voyage they had grumbled about his strictness and rebelled against his discipline, yet now they turned to him as their protector, quite sure that if he gave his word, he would never desert them.

"As God's my witness," he said to them, "you shall find me waiting for you, dead or alive. And if you find not my ships, you shall find their ashes. For I will fight with the galleons if it come to extremity. I will never run."

It was early December when he saw them leave, four hundred men in five small boats, and it was February before the Indian runner reached him with news, weeks of torturing anxiety when he cruised up and down the coast. In an attempt to distract his mind, he began to go ashore to hunt for medicinal plants and herbs, noting their description and uses night by night in his journal. On one of these expeditions, he heard a rumor that turned him cold with wretchedness. An English force was said to have stormed a Spanish town and two of the leaders had been killed. He tried to drag more information out of the Indians but they turned sullen and he knew no more for three long weeks. Then the messenger brought Keymis's letter and confirmed the frightening rumor. There had been a battle. They had sacked the township of San Thomé and Wat was dead. The gay, willful boy who had been so dear to him and Bess lay buried before the high altar of a jungle church.

Walter's grief was terrible. And in addition there was the racking uncertainty as to what had actually happened. Why had they attacked the Spaniards when he had expressly forbidden it? Had they reached the mine or not? There were still weeks to get through before Keymis returned. He still cruised up and down. It kept the men healthy and occupied, but he could concentrate on nothing. The journal was put aside. He would pace up and down the gallery of his ship questioning God in anger and desperation—why had He not let the fever kill him, instead of wrecking everything he had planned to do?

A month after his letter, Keymis returned and saw with love and pity that his leader had grown old. Sorrow at his son's death had turned his hair white. Walter still held himself upright and proud, but he was wretchedly thin and the gray-blue eyes were bright with fever in the gaunt face. At first he greeted Keymis kindly and affectionately. He took him to dine and sup with him in the *Destiny*, but afterward the questions began. What had happened? Why had he disobeyed his strict orders? How had he lost two hundred and fifty men out of his four hundred?

Stumblingly Keymis tried to explain. The township of San Thomé had proved to be nearer than they had expected. They had sailed close to it in the darkness and in the dawn had found themselves very near to the settlement they had believed to be still ahead of them.

Walter could not listen quietly. He paced up and down with a restless broken stride. "Go on, man, go on," he said impatiently. "What then?"

"The Spaniards made a surprise attack on us. The men were thrown into confusion."

"Could you not have rallied them and escaped into the forest?"

"It was your son who rallied them. He shouted to them to follow him. He cried out, 'Come on, my hearts! This is the mine that you must expect. They that look for any other are fools!' They made a rush that carried them into the town. A group of pikemen stood drawn up to receive them." It was the first time Keymis had spoken of Wat's reckless courage, and the look on his chief's face daunted him.

With a wretched clarity Walter realized that it was his son's wild action that had, in part at least, caused the disaster. It did not bear thinking of. He said harshly, "They fought and he was mortally wounded. I know that. Go on."

"You know how much the men loved him. They were maddened by his death and they carried all before them. The Spanish garrison was driven out and the town was taken."

"Why did you stay there? Why not go on to the mine? You knew better than anyone that was my only hope. To bring back the gold was the only proof of my good faith to the king. Who will believe now that I did not lie to him simply to regain my freedom?"

Slowly the truth came out. Keymis had lost his head. His men had been rebellious and muttering against him. At the moment of crisis he had been unable to come to a decision and men from the defeated Spanish garrison were still sniping at them from the surrounding forest.

"I had begun to wonder whether after all these years we would ever find the mine," he said desperately.

"A blind man could have found it from the observations you made yourself on your last expedition," was the cutting reply.

"I was afraid that after what had happened it would be heavily guarded."

"Seeing that my son was dead, do you think I would have cared if you had killed a hundred Spaniards so long as you had reached the mine? Or did you expect to find me dead on your return? Is that it? Then there would have been no one to answer to, no one you would have had to face."

"It was not like that," pleaded Keymis. "I never thought of such a thing. You know what the men were like, vicious, difficult to control, and I was alone in command. George Ralegh had taken some of the most reliable to explore further up the Orinoco."

The only one among them who had shown any spirit or strength of mind, and he had thought him too young to be placed in command!

Keymis was still speaking. "We knew too that you had been betrayed. We found among the governor's possessions the very list of ships and armaments in your own hand, which His Majesty must have given to Count Gondomar. It had been sent to Spain and forwarded from Madrid."

The knowledge of the treachery surrounding his admiral and the strong rumor that a large Spanish force was marching against them had sapped the last ounce of Keymis's willpower.

Walter was swept by such a hurricane of anger and despair he would not listen to excuses or explanations. He himself in the same circumstances would have let nothing stand in his way. He lashed Keymis with angry, scornful words. He thrust aside contemptuously his offer to write to the council in England and take the whole responsibility for their failure on his own shoulders. "It is I who will be blamed, I on whom the whole burden of your folly will rest. Do you think they will listen to you in London? And if they do, you must answer for yourself. I will take no part in it."

Keymis, in his misery at having failed the man he loved and had served faithfully for so many years, did not see the feverish glitter in Walter's eyes, did not realize how near he was to breaking down, did not remember that Walter had never in his life left a friend or dependent to face judgment alone. He only heard the contemptuous voice destroying the years of friendship between them, and he was filled with despair. He said quietly, "I understand. You have made it very clear. I know now what course I must take," and went out of the cabin.

Walter, still walking up and down, still shaking with anger, thought he heard a shot. He called through the door to know what had happened and Keymis's voice, cheerful and reassuring, called back that he had accidentally fired off his gun while cleaning it. A few minutes later one of the men burst in, begging him to come at once.

Walter followed him to Keymis's cabin. He was lying across the bed, blood soaking into the blanket, the knife still in his breast, the gun that had failed him fallen to the floor. At that terrible moment Walter could feel no pity, only a baffled rage. Not only had Keymis ruined him, but by killing himself he had removed the only witness to his good faith. They would believe he had committed suicide in remorse at his treachery toward the king, and who would they hold responsible for that treachery but himself?

The chaplain obstinately refused to read the burial service over a man who had taken his own life. Keymis was thrust hurriedly into the dry, crumbling earth while Walter watched with an unrelenting face.

Keymis's suicide depressed everyone. Rumors ran from one to another of the men. Perhaps their admiral had killed his friend himself to prevent him revealing some dark treason. Those who had been up the Orinoco were telling fantastic stories to those who had remained behind.

A hopeless spirit of defeat possessed the officers when they gathered around the council table that same evening to discuss what they should do next. Walter's self-control gave way. He broke out passionately: "I will take every man who will follow me. I will go up the river and look for the mine myself."

There was dead silence while they looked at him, horrified, and he went on speaking more wildly in his despair. "My son is gone. What is there left to me but my honor? There need be only one basket of the ore to prove I was not lying to the king."

But they would not agree. They were afraid now of what James would do when they returned home. They would suffer with their leader for disobeying orders and attacking the Spaniards. They argued with him. He grew even more desperate, talking wildly of lying in wait for the treasure fleet or of attacking Mexico, where the silver ships were loaded. At last, spent and exhausted, he realized his own folly and gave in. He agreed to abandon Guiana and sail north to Newfoundland for refitting and revictualing the ships before the long journey home.

Left alone, he forced himself to write a careful, detailed report to Sir Ralph Winwood and then steeled his courage to what in all these weeks he had not been able to do. He had implored Winwood to tell Bess of their son's death, but in his heart he knew that she must not hear it from anyone but himself.

"I was loath to write because I knew not how to comfort you: and God knows I never knew what sorrow meant till now." It was difficult to find the words, his mind was so distracted. "Comfort your heart (dearest Bess), I shall sorrow for us both. . . . My brains are broken and it is a torment for me to write and especially of misery. . . . The Lord bless and comfort you that you may bear patiently the death of your valiant son."

He signed and sealed the letter and sat staring into the blank future. He had hoped for much from this venture, hoped to return successful, his good name restored, his position assured, and what was the reality? Their loved son was dead. There was no gold, no possibility of achieving his dream of empire; he was returning more completely ruined than he had ever been. The pain he had suppressed became unendurable. He broke the letter open and wrote a postscript, pouring out his heart to her, telling her of Keymis and repeating over and over again that she was his only comfort, that the thought of her had strengthened his heart and that without it he would not have been able to live.

Sailing toward the north, he tried to think constructively. Perhaps they could winter in Newfoundland and return for another attempt at Guiana in the spring? The one profit Keymis had brought out of San Thomé was a large supply of tobacco. It would pay their way. But one by one his captains deserted him. As far as they could see, only ruin awaited their admiral in England, and they did not intend to share it.

In the cold winds and snow near Newfoundland, where the floating icebergs gleamed green through the freezing mists, his fever left him at last. His men, though they complained of coughs and colds, were no longer dying. There was an attempted mutiny, but Walter proved that, despite everything, he had not lost his courage or his authority.

As they approached land, it came to his ears that as soon as *Destiny* was hauled up on the beach for cleansing, a hundred of the men were planning to desert and plunder the richest of the English merchantmen in the harbor, afterwards making their getaway in a stolen boat. He forestalled them by abruptly changing course for England, and when tumult immediately broke out, he faced the mutineers boldly while they abused and threatened him.

To the astonishment of his nephew, who had believed his uncle a broken and defeated man, Walter charmed them into giving up their intention, promising that he would land them in Ireland, where they could be free and would not suffer any harm on his account. One of them stared at him, saying with a sneer, "You are a fool, Sir Walter. If you return poor as you are with nothing, you will be despised and punished for your failure."

"Perhaps," he answered dryly. "But even if I am to become no more than a beggar in the streets, I would still not turn robber, nor would I abuse the confidence and commission of His Majesty."

The crisis was over and the course set for England, but he still could not trust them. The strain and the sleepless nights when he remained wakeful and on watch with his gun beside his pillow brought on an attack of the pleurisy from which he had suffered in the Tower. During the nights and days of pain, he lay listening to the familiar sounds of the ship, the creaking of the timbers, the distant call of the watch, the whistle of the wind in the rigging, the slap of the waves against the bows. *Destiny* was sound and seaworthy, and if he were to follow the example of his captains and turn pirate, he could be rich in a few months. If he were to sail her to France or Denmark, he could sell her and her contents and live comfortably on the proceeds. These were the temptations that went through his mind and were rejected utterly.

He owed allegiance to England, however untrustworthy her king. He still had to provide for Bess and Carew, left almost penniless. He had given his promise to Arundel and Pembroke and his honor was still unbroken. Above all, there lived within him that unquenchable spirit that would not let him acknowledge defeat or failure. He would not creep away like a beaten dog. After all, what could they do to him? He was not the first man to fail in a difficult enterprise. He could still face whatever was coming to him with courage and dignity.

18 : *"A Star at which the World hath gazed"*

—The Attorney General

It was June before Walter dropped anchor in Plymouth harbor and was rowed ashore. After the months in tropic heat and icy cold, England had never looked more lovely, the fields cool and green, roses blooming in the gardens, and everywhere the sweet scents of summer.

Bess caught her breath at sight of him. He was so thin and white, he looked the ghost of himself. Her joy at having him back beside her was mingled with sharp anxiety. There was so much that he had to know. Exaggerated rumors of all that had taken place in Guiana had preceded him, truth mixed with lies. At a meeting of the Privy Council hastily summoned to decide his fate, the Spanish ambassador had talked loudly of Ralegh's "murders, sackings, pillage, and burnings, such as never were seen even in time of war." There were some who vigorously denied the charges, but they were few. James, frightened by Gondomar's threats, had issued a Proclamation condemning Walter for having "maliciously broken and infringed the peace" and expressing utter detestation of his "scandalous and enormous outrages" committed against the king's "dear brother, the King of Spain." To make the situation even worse, Sir Ralph Winwood, the friend in whom he had trusted, who had known all the details of what had been agreed between him and James, had died nearly six months before.

It was alarming news, but for a while he was too exhausted to take any immediate action to clear himself. He and Bess had gone through too much. It was hard to speak of Wat, the boy they had both loved so dearly, and not even to his beloved wife could he talk of Keymis and his tragic suicide. It was some days before he felt strong enough to sit a horse. Then they set out for London with the firm determination to state his case and fight for justice. They had not ridden twenty miles before they were met by Sir Lewis Stukeley with orders for Walter's arrest.

Stukeley was vice-admiral of Devon, a nephew of Richard Grenville and a distant relative whom Walter had often treated kindly in the past. He had never yet had cause to fear treachery from one of his own kinsmen and so they returned quietly to Plymouth. Stukeley treated him with consideration, leaving him comparatively free while he himself went aboard the *Destiny*, still loaded with the valuable tobacco. When Sir Walter was safely locked up, he thought cunningly, he could sell the tobacco at a good profit to himself.

The loyal Sam King was urging Walter to escape. There was a French ship lying at anchor and the captain was willing to carry him to France. In a few hours he could be a free man. Walter was difficult to persuade. He had not returned to England simply to run away at the first sign of trouble. Reluctantly, he yielded to Bess's tearful entreaties.

On a warm, moonless July night, he was rowed with Captain King across the dark waters of the harbor. The ship was already faintly visible when he knew it was impossible. He could not run like a common criminal fleeing from justice. He ordered the boatman to turn back.

He had regained some of his natural optimism and did not realize how hard James was being driven by lack of money and the Spanish ambassador's constant badgering. The hoped-for gold from Guiana had not materialized. Parliament had obstinately refused to grant the subsidies he needed. There was only one source left, a marriage between the Infanta of Spain and Prince Charles, with the fine fat dowry that would come with it, and Gondomar was demanding as his price the head of Walter Ralegh, preferably to be cut off in Madrid. James twisted and turned and could not make up his mind. Many members of the Privy Council, even those who hated Walter, were disgusted at the idea of any Englishman being sent to a foreign country for punishment. England was not yet the slave of Spain. George Carew was leading a strong party that pleaded for pardon. The whole country was bitterly opposed to the Spanish marriage and sharply critical of James's treatment of a man whom they had grown to respect. James faced a hopeless problem. Why on earth had the wretched man come back, he thought. If only Walter had run away, they could have conveniently slandered him as a treacherous coward and left some other nation to deal with him. Now he had to show both Gondomar and Walter that he knew how to act. He sent a peremptory order to Stukeley that he should convey his prisoner to London as soon as possible.

They set out at once, Walter and Bess with Captain King,

Sir Lewis Stukeley, and a certain French Dr. Manourie who pretended friendship and was easily bribed by Stukeley to act as spy. Manourie knew how to talk intelligently about science and medicine and, having captured the prisoner's interest, he then carefully noted down every word he uttered, however trivial, that might be used against him. Walter was learning caution, but when they rode past Sherborne and he saw the tears in his wife's eyes, he could not stop himself from exclaiming bitterly, "All this was mine and it was taken from me unjustly!"

He had not been deceived by the crafty Frenchman, and he now realized the seriousness of his position. When they reached London, he could be rushed to the gallows without an opportunity to speak in his own defense. Somehow or other he must gain time. On the road to Salisbury he thought out a plan and persuaded Manourie to play a part in it. When they were lodged at the inn, he feigned sickness of such a severe kind that Stukeley, a nervous little man terrified of plague, called in the town physicians. Puzzled by a patient who looked as if he were on the point of death, they were easily persuaded to agree with Dr. Manourie that he was too ill to be moved at least for a day or two. Walter knew very well that he would be condemned for his deception when it was discovered, but he was determined not to die unheard, whatever it cost him, and he took a certain sardonic pleasure in seeing how easily he had fooled his captors.

He urged Bess and Captain King to go on ahead, and in the little time granted to him he wrote furiously all the night through. His *Apology* was superb. It was a burning defense of his own and all great men's failures, filled with a rushing indignation and strength like a man going into battle with his sword unsheathed. Was it so strange, he asked, that he should fail, "drawing after me the chains and fetters wherewith I had been thirteen years in the Tower, being unpardoned and in disgrace with my Sovereign?" He stressed again what he had always firmly believed: that Guiana was an English possession taken by himself for Queen Elizabeth at his first expedition in 1595 by voluntary agreement with the native chieftains. James knew that as well as he and had ordered him to go there. How then could he be guilty of trespassing on Spanish property? How could he be condemned for a battle that had been fought when he had been lying sick three hundred miles away? Besides, it was the Spaniards who attacked first. Surely, he pointed out with savage irony, "the ambassador does not esteem us for so wretched and miserable a people as to offer our throats to their swords without any manner of resistance."

His *Apology* written, he made a rapid recovery, and they started out again. In London he was permitted to go to the house in Broad Street where Bess was waiting for him, still not realizing that Stukeley had been especially commanded by the king to spy on his every action. All his friends—Sam King, George Carew, even the queen herself—were urging him to escape, and now for the first time the prospect seemed attractive. He had fulfilled his promise to return. He had written his defense. It would be only folly to stay and let himself be sent to death. The French ambassador, only too anxious to spite Spain, offered a ship. Walter thanked him but preferred not to be obliged to a foreigner. Stukeley promised to arrange everything.

On a misty, dark night in August, a boat took him swiftly down the Thames with Sam King and Stukeley beside him. He was disturbed by the skiff that followed so close on their tail, though Sir Lewis scoffed at his doubts. It aroused the suspicions of the watermen. They refused to row, hanging back even when Captain King pressed more gold on them. Walter began to realize that they would never reach the waiting ship by dawn. He guessed at treachery and ordered them to land at Greenwich. As he stepped out and would have moved quickly away, Stukeley held him back with warm assurances of friendship. In those few seconds the other boat glided up beside them and men leaped out on the bank. With cool triumph Sir Lewis formally arrested Walter and Sam King for seeking to escape justice.

There was a moment of silence in the darkness on that muddy bank. In the flickering light of the boat's lantern, Walter looked down at the man he had thought a friend and knew him for the traitor he was. "Sir Lewis," he said quietly, "these actions will not turn out to your credit." Then he turned away and put a hand on the captain's shoulder. "You need be in fear of no danger, Sam, it is I only who am the mark shot at."

In the early dawn he stood on the cobbled causeway of the Tower in front of the Traitor's Gate while they stripped him of the few personal possessions he had picked up at the last moment: fifty pounds in gold, a grinning little Guiana idol of gold and copper, a silver seal with his own arms engraved on it, his naval officer's gold whistle set with diamonds, charts of Guiana and the river Orinoco, a few jewels, and a gold-framed miniature of his wife, a pitiful remnant of his former grandeur. Stukeley pocketed them all but the miniature. Walter would not let it go out of his hands until the lieutenant of the Tower, who had been a sympathetic onlooker of the degrading little scene, offered to take charge of it for him.

Sam King was shaking his hand, begging to be allowed to stay with him, but the guard roughly forced him away. Through the hazy summer morning the gray stone walls slowly took shape. The damp of the river had set his lame leg aching. Wearily he felt he had never been away. The last two years with their exultation of freedom, their hope and bitter failure, might never have been. The room in which they shut him might have been the same one, with the same thick stone walls, small barred window, and close, chilling atmosphere.

Walter shivered. The fever that had never really left him began once more to creep through him. He knew its symptoms so well: the ache in his body, the flush of heat, the cold that shook him from head to foot, the feverish delirium that made it so difficult to keep his mind under control. Just then he was too tired to do battle any longer, but they had not yet finished with him.

The king had got Walter into prison; now he had to pin a convincing charge on him, and it was not easy. He refused to allow a public trial. Too much might come out about his own double-dealing. Besides, at Winchester years ago Walter had turned the people's minds from hatred to compassion by his steadfast courage and his brilliant defense. There was no doubt that, old and sick as he was, he would rise to it just as splendidly as before. Maddeningly, none of the accusations against him really amounted to anything. The most careful interrogation of his captains and his crews had not revealed treason or disloyalty. Conspiring to escape to France with the intention of harming his country seemed to be promising, but the French ambassador, in answer to close questions as to what Sir Walter was going to do in his land, merely shrugged his shoulders. "Il mangera, il boyera, il ferait bien," he said dryly. "Eat, drink and enjoy himself!" snorted James angrily. They would have to try something else.

Sir Thomas Wilson, who had been one of the meanest of Robert Cecil's spies, was given his orders. He was to be shut up with Ralegh in the Tower to question, probe, and goad him into protest. Walter had always been recklessly outspoken. It should be easy to trap him into saying something disloyal or treasonable toward the king. Wilson got him locked into an upper room, forbidden all visitors, and forced to beg for pen and paper even to write a note to his wife, but he succeeded in nothing else. Walter, awake to the treachery around him, was taking a bitter pleasure in tormenting the mean creature they had put in charge of him.

"In my humble opinion the rack is the only solution for such a man," Wilson wrote indignantly in one of his long, painstaking reports. Every letter between Walter and Bess was scrutinized and copied, but they never contained anything that could be used against him. In the end James could not be bothered to read them. Walter endured this mental torment for a month and then exploded in an angry letter to the king, the blistering sentences making even James feel uncomfortable.

"I find no reason why the Spanish ambassador should complain of me if it were lawful for the Spanish to murder thirty-six Englishmen, tying them back to back and then cutting their throats!"

Wilson had proved no good at all. He was withdrawn, and James looked around for another way out of his dilemma. It was Francis Bacon who found it for him. He pointed out that the prisoner was still under sentence of death and that he had only been allowed to live all these years by the mercy of the king. As soon as that mercy was withdrawn, the former condemnation remained in force.

In one of his famous essays, Bacon had written, "There is little friendship in this world and least of all between equals." Now he proved it. At a private hearing he looked full in the face of the man to whom he had given his solemn word that the king's commission was as good as a pardon and now denied it, telling him that he must die on that old charge of treason, of which by now the whole of England knew him to be innocent.

James was frightened by the fierce public reaction he was stirring up throughout the country. Gondomar was so hated that he hardly dared to ride openly in his carriage. Mud and stones were hurled at "the devil in a dungcart," even though some of the people were caught and flogged for it. Stukeley was shunned by everyone. "Sir Judas" they shouted after him in the streets, and when he complained to the king, James gave him no sympathy. "If I were to hang all who speak ill of you," he said irritably, "all the trees in my kingdom would not be sufficient. Let Ralegh's death be upon your head," he mumbled as he shuffled quickly out of the room. He would not listen to the pleading of George Carew nor that of his queen. He did not even glance at the pathetic appeal that the thirteen-year-old Carew had written out so carefully, begging for the life of "my poor father, sometime honored with many great places of command by the most worthy Queen Elizabeth." The death warrant was prepared.

There was one more formality that Walter had to be dragged from his bed for. On October 28 he was hurried into a boat at the watergate of the Tower. Sick with fever, his clothes pulled on in haste, he could only try and preserve what little strength he had to meet the last condemnation with dignity and pride. The boat shot under London Bridge, past Blackfriars, Durham House, and the Palace of Whitehall. Then he was climbing the steps at Westminster. Standing at the bar where so many men had been judged, he heard all the old charges rolled out by the Clerk of the Court. To be condemned for being a friend to the Spaniard and to die for being their utter enemy seemed the purest irony. He held his aching body erect and heard the attorney general pass judgment in words surely never spoken before of any traitor:

"Sir Walter Ralegh hath been a statesman and a man who in regard of his parts and quality is to be pitied. He hath been a star at which the world hath gazed; but stars may fall, nay they must fall when they trouble the sphere wherein they abide."

"You have been both valiant and wise," began the Lord Chief Justice, "and I doubt not that you retain both these virtues." He saw the prisoner's smile and his calm proud acceptance of his sentence and hurried on to a conclusion.

James decided the sooner it was all over, the better. The next day, October 29, was the Lord Mayor's Show Day. All the pageants and fine shows in the city would keep the crowds away from the scaffold. He hastily signed the warrant and went back to his hunting trips, to his favorites, and to the *Meditations on the Lord's Prayer* that he was writing for his dear George Villiers.

Walter was taken to the Westminster Gatehouse, since the execution was to take place in the old Palace Yard and not at the Tower. He was permitted visitors, and many friends came that evening, thinking to comfort him, and found it quite unnecessary. He was calm and cheerful, jesting with them so merrily that one acquaintance was a little shocked. "Do not carry it with too much bravery," he said, "or your enemies will take exception to it."

Walter was long past caring what his enemies thought. He smiled. "It is my last mirth in this world, my friend; do not grudge it to me. When it comes to the sad parting, you will find me grave enough."

Dr. Tounson, the self-important young dean of Westminster, came bustling in to bring him religious consolation and found the prisoner needed none of his fine words.

"I give God thanks that I have never feared death," Walter said quietly, "and though the manner of it may seem grievous, yet I had rather die so than of a burning fever. After all, the world itself is only a larger prison and every day there are some selected for execution."

The brisk young clergyman could find no answer. He went away promising to return at dawn with the sacrament and leaving Walter to face his worst ordeal, the farewell to his wife. Bess was trembling, but she fought hard to keep back the tears when he drew her to sit beside him, trying to keep her mind off the coming day by talking of Carew's education. "There are many of my possessions still in the *Destiny*," he reminded her. "Get them if you can. They are all I have to leave and I would like the boy to have them." Though he knew she would have little enough, he begged her to help the widows of some of the men who had given him such loyal service. "There is John Talbot's mother also," he went on. "I fear she will be penniless without her son."

Bess broke down into a storm of weeping so that he could scarcely hear what she was saying. "The lords of the council would not listen to my pleading though I went on my knees," she sobbed, "but they have promised that I shall have your body."

"It is well, dear Bess," he said gently, "that you should have the disposal of that dead which living was so often denied to you."

The hour of midnight struck and she had to leave. George Carew was waiting for her. She looked back once, the flickering candlelight chasing away the years and changing him to the brilliant handsome man who had been all her life since she saw him first at Elizabeth's court. Then the door closed.

Some time during the night Walter remembered the verses he had written for her soon after they met. She smiled at him then for writing so sad a love poem. As the lines came back into his mind, he wrote them on the flyleaf of his Bible:

> Even such is Time! who takes in trust
> Our youth, our joys, and all we have,
> And pays us but with earth and dust:
> Who in the dark and silent grave,
> When we have wandered all our ways,
> Shuts up the story of our days.
> But from that earth, that grave, that dust,
> The Lord shall raise me up, I trust.

She would read them and remember and know that his last thoughts had been of her.

He was to die at nine o'clock and time was growing short. He had been allowed some of his clothes and jewelry back. He dressed slowly, gray silk stockings, black taffeta breeches, white shirt. The governor of the Tower had returned to him the miniature of his wife. Walter put the thin gold chain around his neck and thrust the picture inside his shirt, over his heart. Black satin waistcoat, russet doublet, and then the handsome black velvet gown. He smiled at his own vanity in wanting to make as fine a show as possible, just as he had done in the days of splendor. Not much of all that magnificence left to him now, nor of the intellectual pride that had earned him the name of atheist. Such vanities were past. He slipped a diamond ring on his finger, a gift from Elizabeth, a reminder of his years of passionate devotion to her.

When they brought him breakfast, he found himself hungry and ate with good appetite. Afterward he lighted his pipe with a touch of wry humor, since it would undoubtedly annoy the king when it was reported to him. He glanced through the notes he had made. It was the right of every man to speak from the scaffold, and on this his last public appearance, he was determined to defend himself against the slanders that had blackened his name.

Walter was roused from his thoughts by the tramp of the guard and a shouted command. The time had come, and he went out of his prison and into a square crammed with people. They climbed up on buildings and perched on railings. There were noblemen on horseback and fine ladies at windows. The Lord Mayor down in the city had been deserted.

A big, burly fellow thrust through the guard, holding out a cup, and he took it, drinking a little of the wine.

"Is it to your liking, Sir Walter?"

"It is good drink, friend," he said, smiling, as he handed back the cup, "if a man might but tarry by it."

They had almost to fight their way through the press of people around the scaffold, and he was forced to pause to recover breath. Noticing an old man with an extremely bald head whom the guard were pushing back, he asked him what had brought him out on such a raw morning. "Nothing," said the man, "but to see you and to pray God to have mercy on your soul." Walter thanked him for his goodwill and, with a merry glance at the bald head, pulled off his laced nightcap and tossed it into the eager outstretched hands. "You need this, friend, more than I."

As he mounted the scaffold, the keen wind made him shiver. The sheriffs invited him to come down and warm himself at their fire, but he shook his head. He began to speak and found that his voice was weaker than he had hoped. A wave of feverish giddiness washed over him and for an instant he thought he would faint. Then it passed and with a surge of vitality he began again.

"I thank God heartily that He has brought me into the light to die, and has not suffered me to die in the darkness of the Tower, where I have suffered so much adversity and a long sickness. And I thank God that my fever has not taken me at this time, as I prayed God that it would not."

Point by point he answered the charges that had been brought against him, while the crowd murmured, moved with pity and anger on his behalf. It would have been easy for him to rouse them to fury against the king who was killing him so unjustly, but loyalty to the crown had been part of his life, no matter who wore it. He dismissed James with a touch of contempt. "What have I to do with kings who am about to go before the King of Kings?"

There was much else, and the vast throng of spectators listened in a hushed silence to the calm, quiet voice. Many of them were moved to tears when he came to the edge of the scaffold asking them to pray with him "to the Great God of Heaven whom I have grievously offended. . . . For a long time my course was a course of vanity. I have been a seafaring man, a soldier, and a courtier, and in the temptation of the least of these there is enough to overthrow a good mind and a good man. So I take my leave of you all, making my peace with God. I have a long journey to make and must bid the company farewell."

It was finished at last. He took off his gown and doublet.

"A Star at which the World hath gazed" : 231

The sharp wind ruffled the curling white hair. Still upright and proud, he looked suddenly young with the frilled shirt open at the throat. He took the ax from the reluctant executioner.

"Let me see it. Do you think I am afraid of it?" He smiled as he tried the edge against his thumb. "This is a sharp medicine, but it is a physician for all diseases."

He refused the blindfold. "Think you I fear the shadow of the ax when I fear not the ax itself?" When he lay down, he said, "When I stretch out my hand, dispatch me." He bent his head in prayer for a moment, then held up his hand. The headsman was trembling and did not move. He stretched out his hand again; the masked figure raised the ax but still held back. There was a moment of unbearable tension before the watching crowd heard his voice ring out loud and sharp in command. "What do you fear? Strike, man, strike!" and the blow fell and fell again. A deep groan rose and swelled through the people, and the executioner as he lifted the head dared not cry out the usual formula, "Behold the head of a traitor!" Instead, someone among the spectators shouted, "We have not another such head to be cut off!"

His body was taken hurriedly into St. Margaret's Church close by, while the men and women lingered in the streets, refusing to be dispersed by the soldiers. An unknown poet among those who watched that day was so deeply moved he went away to write of it:

> Great Heart! Who taught thee so to die?
> Death yielding thee the Victory!
> Where took'st thou leave of life? If here,
> How could'st thou be so far from Fear? . . .
> Farewell! Truth shall this story say,
> We died: Thou only liv'st that Day.

That evening, distracted with grief, Bess wrote to her brother: "The lords have given me his dead body though they denied me his life. . . . God hold me in my wits."

He had not achieved his dream, but he had kept it living within him until the last, an inspiration to others who would follow in the path he had marked out. In his *History* he had written of those rare souls, "those few black swans . . . who behold Death without dread and the grave without fear and embrace both as necessary guides to endless glory." He might have been writing the epitaph for his own unmarked grave.

BIBLIOGRAPHY

Contemporary sources are many and mainly out of reach of the general reader. Ralegh's *History of the World* and his political writings have not been published since 1829, and then not in their entirety. I have gone back to the originals and also drawn from the *Calendar of State Papers*, John Hooker's *History of Ireland* in Holinshed's *Chronicles*, T. B. Howell's *State Trials*, John Aubrey's *Brief Lives*, Thomas Fuller's *Worthies of England*, and many other letters, records, and documents. Ralegh's letters can be found in Edward Edwards's biography of him (1868), and Ralegh's *Guiana* in Hakluyt's *Principal Navigations of the English Nation*. I am indebted to the publications of the Hakluyt Society, particularly Ralegh's journal of his last voyage, edited by Sir R. H. Schomburgk, who sailed over his route at the same season of the year and testified to the accuracy of his seamanship, especially bearing in mind the navigational instruments of his time.

Books of interest to the general reader are:

Akrigg, George P. *Jacobean Pageant or The Court of King James I*. Cambridge, Mass.: Harvard University Press, 1962.

Bowen, Catherine Drinker. *The Lion and the Throne: The Life and Times of Sir Edward Coke*. Boston: Atlantic Monthly Press, 1957.

———. *Francis Bacon: Temper of a Man.* Boston: Atlantic Monthly Press, 1963.
Bradbrook, Muriel C. *The School of Night.* New York: Cambridge University Press, 1936. Reprint. New York: Russell and Russell, 1965.
Bradford, Ernle. *The Wind Commands Me: A Life of Sir Francis Drake.* New York: Harcourt, Brace & Jovanovich, Inc., 1965.
Burton, Elizabeth. *The Pageant of Elizabethan England.* New York: Charles Scribner's Sons, 1958.
———. *The Pageant of Stuart England.* New York: Charles Scribner's Sons, 1962.
Churchill, Sir Winston. *History of the English-Speaking Peoples.* Vol. II, *The New World.* New York: Dodd, Mead & Company, 1957.
Clark, Eleanor G. *Ralegh and Marlowe.* New York: Fordham University Press, 1941. Reprint. New York: Russell and Russell, 1965.
Handover, P. M. *The Second Cecil.* New York: Fernhill House, Ltd., 1959.
Harlow, Vincent T. *Ralegh's Last Voyage.* London: Argonaut Press, 1932.
Harrison, George B. *The Life and Death of Robert Devereux, Earl of Essex.* London: George Routledge & Sons, Ltd., 1917.
———. *The Elizabeth Journals.* London: George B. Routledge & Sons, Ltd., 1938.
———. *A Jacobean Journal.* London: George B. Routledge & Sons, Ltd., 1941.
Irwin, Margaret. *That Great Lucifer: A Portrait of Sir Walter Raleigh.* New York: Harcourt, Brace & Jovanovich, Inc., 1960.
Jenkins, Elizabeth. *Elizabeth the Great.* New York: Coward, McCann & Geoghegan, Inc., 1956.
———. *Elizabeth and Leicester.* New York: Coward, McCann & Geoghegan, Inc., 1962.
Latham, A. M. C. *Poems: Sir Walter Ralegh.* London: The Muses Library, 1951.
McElwee, William. *The Wisest Fool in Christendom: The Reign of King James I and VI.* New York: Hillary House Publishers, Ltd., 1958.
Mattingly, Garrett. *Armada.* Boston: Houghton Mifflin Company, 1959.
Neale, John E. *Queen Elizabeth First.* New York: St. Martin's Press, Inc., 1959.
———. *The Elizabethan House of Commons.* Baltimore: Penguin Books.
Oakeshott, Walter T. *The Queen and the Poet.* New York: Fernhill House, Ltd., 1960.
Quinn, David B. *The Voyages and Colonial Enterprises of Sir Humphrey Gilbert.* The Hakluyt Society, 1940.
———. *Ralegh and the British Empire.* Mystic, Connecticut: Lawrence Verry, Inc., 1947.

Rowse, Alfred L. *The Elizabethans and America.* London: Macmillan & Company, Ltd., 1959.
———. *The England of Elizabeth.* New York: The Macmillan Company, 1968.
———. *Ralegh and the Throckmortons.* London: Macmillan & Company, Ltd., 1962.
———. *Sir Richard Grenville of "The Revenge."* New York: Fernhill House, Ltd., 1962.
Strachey, Lytton. *Elizabeth and Essex.* New York: Harcourt, Brace & Jovanovich, Inc., 1969.
Thompson, Edward. *Sir Walter Ralegh.* London: Macmillan & Company, Ltd., 1935.
Waldman, Milton. *Sir Walter Ralegh.* London: William Collins Sons & Co., Ltd., 1943.
Williams, Norman L. *Sir Walter Raleigh.* Baltimore: Penguin Books, 1962.
Wilson, John Dover. *Life in Shakespeare's England.* Baltimore: Penguin Books, 1944.

INDEX

Alençon, Duc d', 21, 27, 40–1
Alleyn, Edward, 68, 196
Anne of Denmark, 179–80, 190–1, 193, 200, 221, 225
Antelope, 138, 147
Apology, 220–1
Aremberg, Count d', 147
Ark Ralegh (*Ark Royal*), 68, 70, 76, 180
Arundel, Earl of, 201, 216
Ascham, Roger, 18
Ashton, Roger, 169
Azores, 89–90, 95, 121

Babington, Anthony, 65
Bacon, Francis, 140, 199–200, 224–5
Bark Ralegh, 46, 49
Barlow, Arthur, 52

Bath, 125, 189
Beaumont, Francis, 196
Berreo, Antonio de, 102
Black Dog, 58
Blackfriars, 93, 225
Blackwater River, 33, 82, 204
Boleyn, Anne, 65, 70
Book of the Ocean to Cynthia, The, 94
Boyle, Lord, 203–4
Broad Street, 193, 221
Brooke, Elizabeth, 88; *see also* Cecil, Lady
Brooke, George, 154
Brooke, Henry, *see* Cobham, Lord
Brydges, Elizabeth, 86
Burghley, Lord, 20, 28–9, 38, 40–1, 43, 65, 71–3, 83, 88, 110, 119, 129, 144, 146, 186
Byrd, William, 66

Cadiz, 74, 111–13, 117–20, 163, 184
Cape Verde, 26, 203, 206
Carew, George, 13, 25, 31, 51, 93, 111, 118, 175, 179, 205, 219, 221, 225, 227
Carew, Richard, 57
Carr, Robert, 180, 186–8, 191, 194
Cecil, Robert, 29, 72–3, 76, 88, 91, 94–6, 109–10, 112, 119, 121, 126–7, 129–31, 133–4, 139–41, 144, 146–8, 151–2, 154–7, 163, 166, 168, 170, 175, 177, 179, 183, 186, 189, 192, 195–6, 223
Cecil, Lady, 112, 119, 126
Cecil, Will, 112, 126, 137–9, 141
Cecil, William, see Burghley, Lord
Champernowne, Henry, 5–8
Chapman, George, 97, 110
Charles, Prince, 180, 195, 219
Chatham, 41, 91, 120
Christian, King of Denmark, 180, 204
Cobham, Lord, 126–7, 130–1, 133–4, 147–8, 154–7, 160, 162–7, 170–2, 176
Coke, Edward, 160, 162, 164–6
Cork, 31, 33–4
Cornwall, 46, 56–7, 75, 92, 97, 109, 111

da Gama, Vasco, 51
Dartmoor, 6, 56
Dee, John, 44, 51
Deptford, 17, 38, 44, 68, 184
Destiny, 195, 200–3, 206, 210, 215–16, 218, 227
Devereux, Robert, see Essex, Earl of
Devon, 5, 12–13, 23, 25, 32, 39, 43, 56–7, 75, 95, 97, 101, 159, 163, 201, 218

Dorothy, 49, 58
Dorset, 88, 96
Dover, 76, 198
Drake, Francis, 12, 24, 36, 38, 44, 61, 74–6, 117
Drayton, Michael, 68
Dreadnought, 114
Dudley, Robert, see Leicester, Earl of
Dulwich, 196, 198
Durham House, 50, 52, 86, 93, 97, 128, 133, 135, 148, 154, 196, 225

Elizabeth, 58
Elizabeth, Princess (daughter of James I), 180, 190–1
Elizabeth I, Queen of England, 6–7, 10, 13, 18, 20–1, 23–31, 35–6, 38–46, 49–52, 54–6, 58, 60, 64–8, 70–6, 78–9, 81–4, 86–90, 92–7, 102, 108–11, 113, 116–21, 124–7, 129–34, 141–2, 144, 146–8, 152–3, 156, 163, 166, 168, 184, 186, 195–6, 221, 225, 228–9
Essex, Countess of, 27
Essex, Earl of, 70–4, 76, 79, 81, 83–4, 89, 97, 109, 111–35, 140–1, 144, 146, 153, 158, 169
Exeter, 9, 15, 100

Falcon, 24–7
Fawkes, Guy, 176
Fayal, 122, 124
Flying Joan, 206
Frederick, Elector of the Palatine, 189–90
Frobisher, Martin, 24, 76, 92, 117

Gascoigne, George, 19–20
Gheerhaerts, Marc, 137
Gilbert, Adrian, 7, 23

Gilbert, Humphrey, 5–7, 17, 19, 23–5, 27, 30–1, 35, 45–6, 48–9, 57, 184
Gilbert, John (brother of Humphrey Gilbert), 7, 57, 95
Gilbert, John (son of Humphrey Gilbert), 100
Gilbert, Otho, 7
Gilbert, Ralegh, 184
Globe Theatre, 129, 132, 142
Golden Hind, 38
Gomera, 205–6
Gondomar, Count, 199, 201, 205, 212, 217–19, 224–5
Gorges, Arthur, 13, 51, 93, 121, 123, 175, 180, 182–3
Gorges, Fernando, 133
Gray's Inn, 18, 200
Greenwich, 17, 54, 65, 67, 70, 83, 222
Grenville, Richard, 58, 76, 88–90, 114, 117, 218
Grey, Lord, 29, 31–2, 35–6, 82
Guiana, 98–101, 109–12, 117–18, 125, 138, 179, 184–5, 191–5, 198, 200, 214–15, 271, 219, 221–2
Gunpowder Plot, 176–8

Hakluyt, Richard, 14, 51, 68
Halder, Joseph, 67
Hampton Court, 41, 186
Harington, John, 151
Hariot, Thomas, 44–5, 50, 58, 61, 63, 68, 71, 97–9, 110, 175, 179
Harvey, George, 157, 173, 175–6
Hatton, Christopher, 18, 20
Hawkins, John, 12, 44, 74, 76, 95, 117
Hay, James, 169
Hayes, Edward, 46, 48
Hayes Barton, 5, 15, 49–50, 81

Henry VIII, King of England, 16, 28, 64–5, 127, 131, 146, 148
Henry, Prince of Wales, 177, 180, 182–91, 194
History of the World, 188, 191, 193–4, 232
Howard, Catherine, 65–6
Howard, Charles, 75–6, 88, 100, 111–13, 116–17, 125, 148
Howard, Henry, 119, 144, 146–7, 152, 154, 158, 170, 175, 177, 186, 194
Howard, Mary, 86
Howard, Thomas, 88–9, 111–12, 120, 124, 128

Infanta of Spain, 195, 219
Islington, 19, 195–6

James I, King of England, 131–2, 144, 146–54, 158, 160, 162–5, 168, 172–3, 176, 179–80, 185–91, 194–5, 199–201, 204–5, 212, 214, 218–19, 221, 223–6, 230
Jersey, 138, 141, 144, 147, 154
John and Francis, 206
Jonson, Ben, 142, 198
Judith, 12

Keymis, Lawrence, 51, 97, 100–1, 108, 110, 118, 123, 175, 192, 200, 204, 207–13, 215, 218
Kilcolman Castle, 82, 127
King, Sam, 204, 218–22
Knollys, Henry, 25, 27

Lane, Ralph, 58
Leicester, Earl of, 18–20, 23, 27–8, 35, 38, 40–2, 60, 70, 76, 79, 144
Lennox, Earl of, 147
Limehouse, 17, 24
Lion, 58, 114

240 : INDEX

Lisbon, 92, 165
Lismore Castle, 81, 204
London, 6, 12, 15, 17–18, 23, 32, 36–7, 50–2, 57–8, 65, 76, 83, 91, 97, 101, 112, 121, 124, 126, 129, 138, 141, 147, 149, 152, 155, 158, 173, 193, 212, 218–21

Madrid, 25, 201, 212, 219
Manoa, 98–9, 102, 106–8
Marlowe, Christopher, 67, 86, 97
Martinez, Johannes, 98
Mary, Queen of Scots, 7, 64–6, 131
Mary Rose, 114
Mary Spark, 58, 138
Mary Tudor, 9, 89
Medina Sidonia, Duke of, 78, 116
Mermaid Tavern, 142, 196
Middle Temple, 17–18
Morequito, 106–7

Newfoundland, 3, 14, 26, 46, 214–15
Nonpareil, 115
Norfolk, Duke of, 146
Northampton, Earl of, see Howard, Henry
Northumberland, Earl of, 86–7, 97, 110, 176, 178–9, 184
Nottingham, Earl of, see Howard, Charles

Oriel College, 10, 12
Orinoco River, 99, 104, 106–8, 192, 205, 208, 212–13, 222
Ormonde, Earl of, 30, 33–5
Oxford, 6, 10, 12–15, 18, 36, 44, 51, 182, 198
Oxford, Earl of, 28, 43

Panama, 90, 98
Paris, 10, 51, 68, 84, 198

Parliament, 15, 57, 64, 138–9, 142, 176, 179, 195, 219
Pembroke, Earl of, 170, 201, 216
Percy, Algernon, 184
Percy, Henry, see Northumberland, Earl of
Perrot, John, 28
Perrot, Thomas, 28
Pett, Peter, 17, 44, 184
Pett, Phineas, 184, 195, 198
Philip II, King of Spain, 25, 74, 111, 117, 119, 163, 218
Pizarro, Francisco, 14, 98–9
Plymouth, 25, 27, 44, 52, 58, 67, 75, 92, 100, 121, 138, 148, 201–3, 217–18
Portsmouth, 29–30

Rainbow, 114–15
Ralegh, Bess Throckmorton, 84, 86, 88–90, 91, 93–4, 96–9, 101, 109–10, 112, 125–6, 138, 149, 156, 163, 171–2, 175–6, 182–3, 186–9, 191–3, 196, 201–2, 207, 209, 214–21, 224, 227–8, 232
Ralegh, Carew (brother of Walter Ralegh), 7, 57
Ralegh, Carew (son of Walter Ralegh), 176, 182, 186, 195–6, 198, 202, 216, 225, 227
Ralegh, George, 204, 208, 212, 215
Ralegh, Walter (father of Walter Ralegh), 5–6, 8–9, 19, 100
Ralegh, Catherine (mother of Walter Ralegh), 7–9, 100
Ralegh, Wat, 98, 101, 109, 112, 119, 125–6, 137–8, 149, 156, 163, 171–2, 175, 177, 182, 186, 198, 202, 204, 207–12, 214, 218
Report of the Truth of the Fight about the Azores, 90
Repulse, 113–14

Revenge, 76, 89–90, 114
Roche, Lord, 33–4
Roebuck, 58, 75, 92, 95, 138

St. Andrew, 114–15
St. Matthew, 114–15
Saint Michael, 124
St. Philip, 114–15
St. Thomas, 114–15
Salisbury, Earl of, *see* Cecil, Robert
San Thomé, 209–10, 215
Savoy, Duke of, 179, 188
Shakespeare, William, 97, 129, 132, 169, 190, 196
Sherborne, 96–7, 101, 109–10, 118, 125–6, 141–2, 156, 159, 175–6, 182–3, 186–8, 191, 220
Sidney, Philip, 23, 28, 40, 60–1, 83
Somerset, Earl of, *see* Carr, Robert
Southampton, Earl of, 97, 124, 134
Spanish Armada, 74–6, 78, 88, 111, 116–17, 144, 163, 184
Spenser, Edmund, 82–3, 127, 204
Squirrel, 46
Star, 206
Stuart, Arabella, 147, 160
Stukeley, Lewis, 218–22, 225
Sully, Duc de, 141
Surrey, Earl of, 146
Swiftsure, 114

Talbot, John, 126, 175, 204, 206, 227
Tarleton, Richard, 60
Thames River, 12, 16–17, 38, 41, 44, 50, 68, 93–4, 133, 175, 178, 190, 193, 200, 221
Theobolds, 186

Throckmorton, Arthur, 84, 90–1, 94, 112, 116, 232
Throckmorton, Bess, *see* Ralegh, Bess
Throckmorton, Nicholas, 84
Topiawari, 106–8, 207
Tower of London, 17, 56, 93–6, 134, 156–8, 166, 173, 175–6, 178–9, 182, 185–6, 188–9, 192–4, 198, 204, 216, 222–3, 225–6, 228
Trinidad, 102, 108
Triumph, 76
Tyger, 58
Tyrone, Earl of, 127, 130

Victory, 76
Villiers, George, 195, 226
Virginia, 75, 87–8, 98, 184, 190

Waad, William, 158–9, 176, 179
Walsingham, Francis, 20, 29, 38, 40, 64–5, 74, 76, 144
Wanstead, 23, 28
Warspite, 112, 114, 121
Wedel, Leopold von, 52, 54
Westminster Abbey, 15, 153, 158, 196, 204, 225–7
Whidden, Jacob, 99–100
White, John, 58, 63, 75, 87
Whitehall, 6, 16, 18, 27, 36, 41, 46, 50, 120, 124, 225
William of Orange, 41, 60
Wilson, Thomas, 223–4
Winchester, 158–9, 176, 223
Windsor, 41, 155–6
Winwood, Ralph, 195, 200–1, 205, 214, 218
Wolsey, Cardinal, 12, 16

Youghal, 81–2

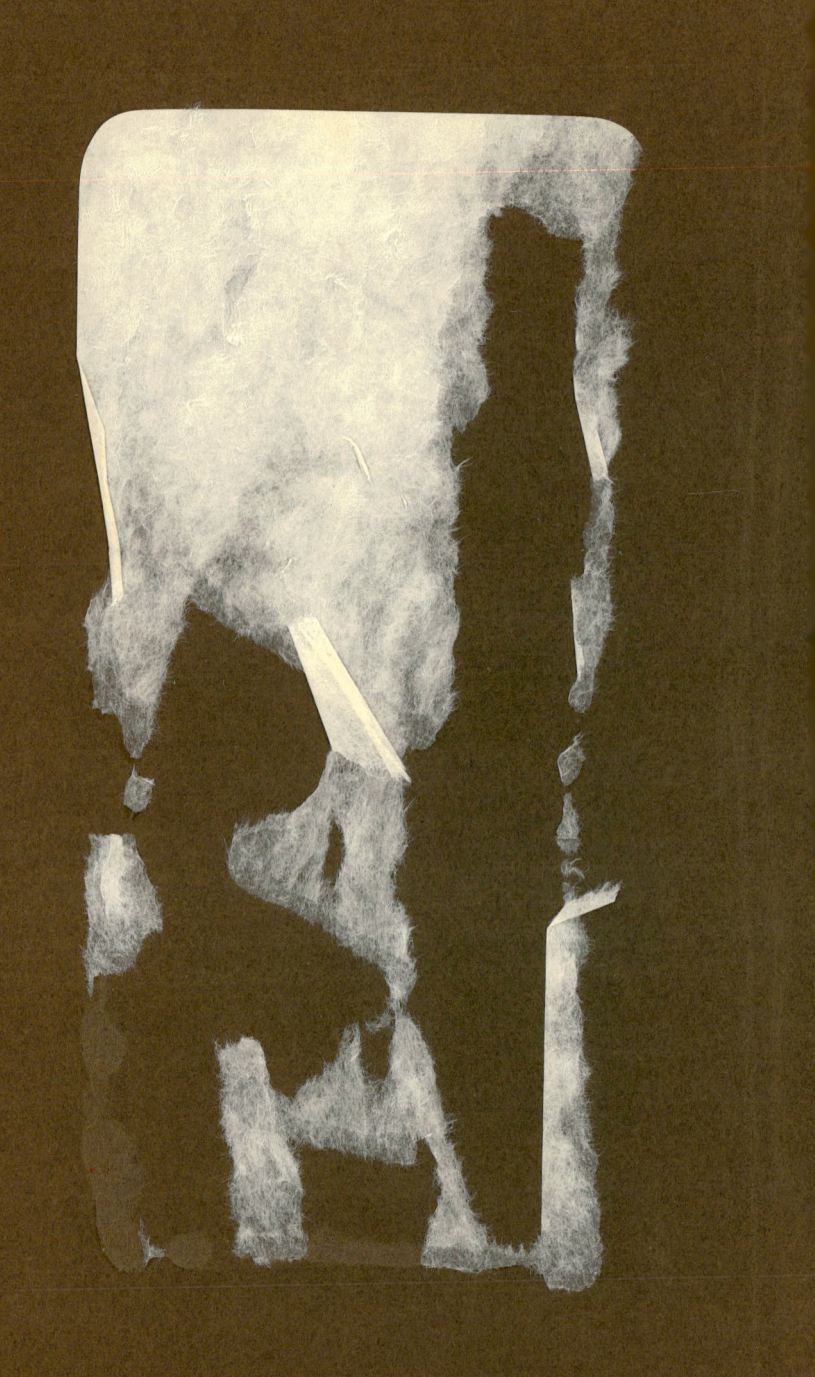